INTERRUPTED SUMMER

ERIC GILLIES BERNARDEZ

KS

Kravitz & Sons
INNOVATORS IN PUBLISHING, MARKETING AND ADVERTISING

Kravitz and Sons LLC
1301 Farmville Blvd, Suite 104
Greenville, NC 27834

Published by Kravitz and Sons LLC.

ISBN: 979-8-89639-263-7 (sc)
ISBN: 979-8-89639-264-4 (e)

Library of Congress Control Number: 2025909504

TABLE OF CONTENTS

To the Philippine Eagle Foundation who are working to save the endangered Philippine Eagle.

PROLOGUE

A farmer in the town of Santa Teresa in the Sierra Madre Mountains of the Philippines discovered tubers that were found to be an excellent stimulant for grain production. He had unearthed them by accident while he was trying to divert more water into his irrigation canal. Believing that the exposed tubers were the cassava root crop he was familiar with, he harvested as much as he could carry, and planted them next to his corn farm.

Months passed. To his amazement, the farmer noticed that the corn plants near the tubers had shown dramatic improvement in their growth and were becoming much more productive than the rest of his crop. He realized that the roots were not of the edible cassava variety after all, but that they seemed to be a good source of cheap and excellent fertilizer for his plants.

Word of the mysterious roots spread like wildfire. Farmers jostled against each other to harvest and plant the remaining tubers next to their corn plots. Unfortunately, their hopes of enhancing, let alone doubling their grain production were dashed when they discovered that the tubers could not be propagated fast enough to replenish those that were dug out earlier. The grain growers realized that they might not be able to produce enough of the miracle fertilizer for their farms on a continuous cycle if they could not grow the roots fast enough to meet their immediate needs.

Anticipating the possibility of such a beneficial discovery, the Farmers' Cooperative Association of Santa Teresa asked the government to spearhead a study to determine the feasibility of large-scale, commercial propagation of the tubers. Cheap fertilizer could offer quite a boon, not only for the local grain producers, but for all farmers in the world.

Five years into the project, and with millions of dollars spent, however, the experiments failed to show encouraging results. The consortium struggled to grow the tubers at an acceptable rate of production. Scientists observed that success in growing the roots was a function of their moisture sensitivity. If moisture remained uncontrolled, as had been the case during the past wet seasons, the tubers were susceptible to attack by viruses, fungi, and other root diseases. The frequent typhoons that had caused destruction in the area also played a major role in the debacle. The use of greenhouses to regulate moisture application to the roots of the plants seemed to enhance production, if only they could hold out against the powerful wind gusts accompanying the big storms.

The research program seemed to be headed for failure. One day, a violent typhoon brought the entire research facility to the ground. All of the experimental tubers, chemical reagents, various catalysts, and blends of plant enzymes used in the study were spilled. Scientists and their crews, having experienced the worst of the bad weather in that mid-montane frontier, left the area in a rush. Abandonment of the project was the obvious recourse if they were not able to find a suitable place to relocate for continuing their research.

Rabbits, rodents, wild pigs, and other animals took over the ruined research facilities to search for food. They gobbled up the tubers treated with chemical reagents and enzymes, and ingested some of the laboratory liquids that spilled to the floor during the storm. Meanwhile, a pair of hungry, monkey-eating eagles, nesting not far from there in the Santa Magdalena Rainforest, swooped down from the sky many times to attack and devour the scavengers on the wrecked research facilities' grounds.

Animals that were able to escape the eagles' attacks near the research site, including a family of wild swine, appeared to the local farmers to have died of poisoning.

Following their consumption of tainted prey, the eagles appeared to have mutated into a more aggressive and ferocious subspecies. Their dramatic buildup in size and strength dwarfed other eagles on the island.

The giant, winged predators ventured out of their customary foraging range in the rainforest for the first time. In search of larger prey, wild or domestic, they boldly entered the bustling town of Santa Teresa.

A stroke of luck might have been the reason for the encounter of Marco Vega, an outdoorsman and a biology major, with the giant eagles. It was an odd encounter, as they lived on different mountain ranges. Their paths would cross and cause mayhem when well-meaning hunters of the Sierra Madre Mountains forced the wayward predators out of their rainforest territory, hoping they would resettle in the deeper reaches of the undisturbed northeast mountains. Unbeknownst to the people in the area, the eagles would change their course and end up in the distant Caraballo Mountains to the southwest.

CHAPTER 1
THE FRESHMAN

I'll be in excellent form when I return to school and the gym in eight weeks. For now, I look forward to enjoying my summer break outdoors.

Between classes, Marco Vega crammed through his textbook and lecture notes in preparation for a difficult pre-final exam in General Chemistry II. This would be his last course that day, and his last written test before the upcoming finals. Of all the courses he had enrolled in that semester, chemistry was by far the hardest. He ran his fingers through his hair, stared at the chalkboard, and fumbled for the right answers halfway through his exam. His face was damp with perspiration on that rather cold and foggy afternoon in March of 1972.

"You have five more minutes to submit your answer sheets," instructor Laura Clemente said. She was labelled a "classroom terror" because of her penchant to flunk up to as many as half her class if they failed to clear the high bar she had set.

"With all due respect, Miss Clemente, how can you expect us to finish this kind of exam in just 40 minutes? I've never had a longer or more difficult test than this one," Marco said.

About two thirds of the class echoed his gripe. "Silence, please," she said. "If this classroom is not scheduled for another class in the next period, I'll give you fifteen more minutes to wrap up your exam. Finished or not, I expect all your answer sheets to be on my desk at five fifty. Is that clear?"

Marco took off from the City of Pines University campus and was on his way to the YMCA gym for his martial arts training. Having used all the extra fifteen minutes for the test, he would not make it to the gym on time for the warm-up exercises.

A stranger in Baguio City when he started college there nine months ago, the shy seventeen-year-old freshman knew hardly anyone outside of his school and boarding house. It didn't matter. "I'll have friends when I want them," he once wrote to his younger brother, Toby, who continued to communicate with him from his hometown in San Antonio, Nueva Vizcaya. Loneliness, as he would occasionally experience while living in the city, was not the result of his seclusion. In fact, whether his short-term solitary existence was a bane or boon for him depended on what his predisposition was on those days. Some days he longed for company, while on other days he wanted to be alone.

Several weeks into the semester, Marco decided to spice up his young life by joining a sports club. He enrolled in Shotokan Karate. The intense training and competition he witnessed in the gym during his orientation was enough to convince him that karate was the sport he would like to try.

"When you practice martial arts, or any other physical sport for that matter, you will learn to assert your self-expression, which is important for your development," Dale Romano, a black belt assistant instructor who initially showed him the gym facilities, said. "Keep in mind that concerted physical activities can help manage stress."

"Thanks for those well-founded words," Marco said. "My alternate choice of sport was basketball, which I played throughout my high school years. I decided against it this time because I don't have the proper height to compensate for my just-average foot speed."

Now as he walked past the cathedral, he was particularly cognizant of the time. He had made a habit of gazing at the huge clock below the left spire of the cathedral to reaffirm that he was on time. This time, he knew that he would be late.

The church bells began their toll. A student walking ahead of him stopped to make the sign of the cross and uttered a short prayer. Marco paid no attention and walked past the student, but as he looked back toward the cathedral grounds, he noticed that everyone else in the crowd—students and churchgoers alike—had stopped to pray. Curious as to what was going on around, he strode over to the student who was about to resume walking and said to him, "I'm new in town. Can you please tell me what's taking place here? I mean, the clanging of the bells, and why people stop and pray?"

"It's six o'clock in the evening, and the church bells call for the observance of The Angelus, a prayer of devotion in honor of the Annunciation and Incarnation of the Blessed Virgin Mary," the student said. "City residents who hear the bells stop what they're doing—be it walking or jogging—to celebrate the occasion. Motorists within earshot of the chimes stop their vehicles to commemorate the event unless they're out-of-towners who are unfamiliar with the ritual."

"I thought so. I'm Marco. Thanks for the information."

"And I'm Constante. I'll see you around the campus."

To be sure, Marco went to a Catholic high school in San Antonio and had studied, among other church doctrines, The Angelus; what it represents, and why it's being observed. "I didn't see people in my hometown stop their activities and recite their prayers every time the bell tolls at six in the evening. They probably practice the rite just like they do here, but I haven't really watched them that closely. Perhaps many of them would rather celebrate the event in private, as I have. Regardless, they do a lot of things differently here."

Marco's Lolo (Grandpa) Gil, who was footing all his school bills, wanted him to pursue his college education in Manila, against the youngster's preference for Baguio. Haggling with his Lolo Gil, yet being careful not to disappoint him, Marco ultimately got what he wanted. His arguments were based on Baguio being as good a university town as any in the country, and that his chosen school was one of the leading institutions of learning in the region.

Surrounded by gold and copper mines, Baguio, also known as The City of Pines, is in the province of Benguet, which lies inside the vast Luzon Pine Forests in the Central Cordillera Mountain Range. Towering to almost 1,540 meters above sea level, the city boasts a superb climate that is no doubt the best in the country. It is a unique and inviting urban community that is set in the mountains where exotic florae grow. Motoring to the city by way of the scenic and zigzagging Kennon Road, one of two accesses from the south, tired travelers enjoy the fresh scent of pine trees permeating the cool and invigorating air. The allure of Baguio attracts many visitors all year round, especially during the observance of the holy week and other important holidays.

In the beginning, Kafagway, as Baguio was called then, was populated by the Ibaloi and Kankanaey tribes of the Cordilleras. The early inhabitants named the place Bagiw, or "moss" in English, for the green, succulent plant abundant in the area. The Dominican missionaries later changed the spelling of Bagiw to Baguio, in part because it rhymes with the local word they often hear, bagyo, which means typhoon. Also, the word was perhaps easier for foreigners to pronounce. The occupants of the city now include many other Filipino ethnic groups and immigrants of different nationalities, many of whom have assimilated into the mainstream culture.

A chartered city since 1909, Baguio was designed by American architect and urban planner Daniel H. Burnham during the American occupation. The Mansion House was built for the American governor general as his summer residence to escape the warm, tropical climate in Manila. Camp John Hay, later called John Hay Air Base, was developed for rest and recreation of the members of the U.S. Armed Forces and their dependents.

After the country had gained her independence from the United States in 1946, The Philippine government followed the same tradition of transferring its seat from the capital city to Baguio during the warm months. Though the practice is continued by only the Supreme Court, the sobriquet "Summer Capital of the Philippines" still stands.

The half-hour cathedral chimes were back to life, reminding Marco that it was time to be in the gym. "The warm-ups must be over now. I can't stand showing up in the middle of the workout with all eyes upon me. It's an awkward feeling."

Alvin Arce, a 2nd-degree black belt and the head instructor of the Japan Karate Association in the city, called out everyone who wore a karategi (karate uniform) to line up in formation, shoulder to shoulder, seven across, and seven deep. He led the supplementary drills or workouts—sometimes called limbering exercises, or warm-ups—designed to increase strength, speed, stamina, and help reduce the occurrence of injuries.

Marco crossed the cathedral loop and entered the commercial building through its main entrance. He went down the flights of wooden stairs to the austere but adequately equipped gymnasium that consisted of a basketball court (also used for martial arts activities), a side recess furnished with weights and other equipment for body building and weight lifting, a soda and snack bar, a small office, and an open changing room for karatekas (karate practitioners) to slip in and out of their uniforms.

He was surprised to see the class still in the middle of the warm-ups instead of going through the routine sparring and training drills.

After completing the cooling down exercises, karatekas pounded the heavy canvas bag and the makiwara (striking padded-board anchored to a post). Loud thumps and thuds resonated across the pinewood and concrete gym.

Black belt assistants divided the karate class into groups according to the color of their belts. Under supervision, the white and blue belts practiced kihon (basics) while the brown belts performed kata (forms).

Arce picked Marco to be the first of his several kumite (sparring) partners. He didn't start a conversation with the latter, perhaps an indication that he would convey his response to his tardiness in a different way.

Relax, and don't show fear when sparring with a tough opponent, particularly the head instructor, Marco said to himself. As it stands, karate sparring doesn't call for full contact. But having sparred with Arce many times in the past, and observing his sparring matches with other students, he was reminded not to be careless, and to avoid being the recipient of blows that are likely to land from time to time. He had received his own share of misplaced bare-knuckle punches that bloodied his nose at times, and had witnessed karate students like him getting knocked down when hit by a roundhouse kick to the jaw, or a reverse punch to the solar plexus. Such blows could land by accident on the upper body, even the face at times.

Striking the makiwara repetitively to improve his hand extension and focus, Marco looked impressive with his hand and hip movements. He had shown his skill in hitting the padded board. His black hair, cropped short to comply with the ROTC requirement, complemented his good looks. If he was a bit nervous about his sparring match with Arce, he made an effort to hide it. He waited in front of the makiwara, glancing on occasion across the gym to check on his upcoming opponent, who was still talking to a young man who wanted to join the class. Before long Arce was ready, having been relieved from one of his diverse duties by an assistant.

Following the protocol to uphold the Japanese karate tradition—bowing toward each other with arms clipped on each side of the body, fists half-clenched and ready—Arce opened the sparring match by lunging at Marco, thumping him on the chest with a leading left back fist that the latter didn't see coming. It was followed by a swift roundhouse kick that was blocked by Marco with his raised left arm. His defense was well-executed, to say the least, but he failed to maintain the correct stance in the ensuing skirmish. His feet were too close together, making him vulnerable to the instructor's next move. Arce saw the opening and with a quick and powerful leg stroke, swept Marco off his feet and sent him crashing to the floor.

"Be careful when you shift your feet on the floor or else your next opponent will drop you like a bag of potatoes," Arce said, his words adjunct to a subconscious display of his odd mannerism of nodding his head repeatedly while hovering over the fallen student. "Maintaining the right stance will keep you standing even after receiving a well-placed blow to the body. The key to learning is to keep doing the right technique over and over until it is absorbed in your system and you feel comfortable doing it."

Feeling somewhat chastised as a result of his inattention to an important detail in sparring, Marco, who appeared to have bruised his left elbow when he hit the floor, realized his mistake and said, "It'll be different next time, Alvin. I'll keep working on my footwork."

"Remember that your stance is your strength. A narrow stance weakens you, while a wide one slows you down. I expect to see improvement on your footwork."

Black belt assistant instructor Joey Valle was watching the action. He led Marco to a corner and showed him the proper stance. He also demonstrated how to snap back to it and maintain proper balance after completing a defensive or offensive tussle. He was aware that Marco had earned his brown belt not long ago, and was certainly not a novice by any means; he had perhaps experienced a beginner's slip-up.

Joey exhibited some of the most basic karate techniques, and added his comments at every pause. "Place your feet firmly on the floor: shoulder-width apart, left foot forward facing your opponent with your left knee bent above your left toes, and right foot slightly angled to the right. Shoulders slightly lowered and relaxed, right arm recoiled for attack, and left arm ready for a downward or upward defensive block. You can assail your opponent in a variety of ways: front snap, side thrust, roundhouse kick, lunge and reverse punches—all offensive strikes that one day you'll be proficient at."

Despite the pain in his elbow that cut short his sparring match, Marco duplicated Joey's well-executed onslaught and defensive action against an imaginary opponent. This was not a surprise because brown belt karatekas are expected to be competent with the basic karate techniques. Joey was confident that Marco was a much better student than Arce had given him credit for. In sparring, he wouldn't match up with the black belts, but at least he could beat most of the brown, and all the blue belts in the gym. All he needed to do was avoid making rudimentary mistakes.

At the close of the karate class, Marco and Joey left the gym and walked through the drifting fog that had shrouded the pine and eucalyptus trees, buildings, streets, and the distant hillsides dotted with numerous dwellings. The fog-obscured streetlights seemed eerie as they emitted flickering light in all directions without offering much luminance. Swarms of insects crowded the lampposts.

It was quite cold that evening; the temperature was in the teens—Celsius. They had to walk faster to maintain their body warmth, since neither of them thought of bringing a jacket or a sweater.

When they went past Raymond Lee's Café and Restaurant at the Downtown Plaza Square, Joey told Marco that he waited tables there six days a week. "Mr. Lee, the owner and manager, allows me to work the early shift when I'm scheduled to assist Arce in the gym. It's very nice of Ray, and I'm so grateful for those three or four mornings a week.

Noticing Marco clasping a textbook and other classroom materials, Joey asked, "What university do you go to?"

"I'm a freshman at the City of Pines University."

"Good for you. Where are you from?"

"I'm from San Antonio.

"In Zambales?"

"No, in Nueva Vizcaya. I'll be home during the summer break. I'll miss my karate training and the camaraderie in the gym."

"When are you leaving?"

"After the final exams in two weeks."

"Keep in shape, wherever you are, and perform the karate basics as often as you can."

"I'll be in excellent form when I return to school and the gym in eight weeks. For now, I look forward to enjoying my summer break outdoors."

"That's a good way to spend your summer vacation.

"Thanks."

"If you haven't heard the news in the gym today, we were visited by three high-ranking members of the Japan Karate Association: Messrs. Tanaka and Sakai from Tokyo, and Mr.

Takahashi from the headquarters in Manila. Arce took pride in showing them our large membership, and the growing number of black and brown belt karatekas."

"I was late, and I offer no excuses. It would have been an honor for me to meet people like them, who have made big contributions in the field of martial arts. I believe those guys were featured in the book I'm currently reading—the memoir of Arthur Miles that he wrote while he was studying karate in Japan."

"Yes, their remarkable involvement in karate was mentioned in the book. And on the subject of tardiness, it's one of the little lapses that we sometimes cannot avoid. We can't be perfect. Unfortunately, Arce wanted our Japanese guests to meet the entire team that will be sent to compete this coming November in the Japan Karate Association national tournament in Manila. You've been chosen by the panel, of which I am a member, to be one of the competitors to represent the club in the annual karate event."

"Yessss! Thanks for the good news," Marco said, pounding his right fist in the air as he always did when he gets too excited. "To participate in the national karate tournament is a big break for me."

"Congratulations! You've earned it."

"I'm grateful to you, to Alvin Arce, to Dale Romano, and to all those who instilled in me that real progress in martial arts can only be achieved through dedication and hard work."

"The Miles book you are currently reading must be well-worn by now. Years ago, Mr. Takahashi gave an autographed copy to Romano, who read it and passed it on to every black and brown belt in the gym. Arce has the other copy. It's an inspiring book for all students of karate."

"Yes, it is. I'm down to my last two chapters, and I should be able to finish reading it in a week or so. I promised to return the copy to Dale before I leave town."

"See you in the gym in two days."

Joey took a jeepney ride home upon reaching the terminal. "Ingat ka!" (Be careful!) he called out to Marco.

"Salamat!" (Thank you!)

Marco continued to walk to his boarding house through the rough backstreets, in constant watch over his shoulders; mindful of the sights, sounds, and all the commotions around him. Once again, he found himself entrenched in that same nightly scenario he'd become familiar with: people walking through the fog-darkened sidewalks and alleys; taxicabs and jeepneys taking on passengers rushing home with their bayong (woven palm shopping baskets); bars serving San Miguel beer and gin or Tanduay rum, while playing Perry Como's evocative rendition of "For The Good Times," time after time; drivers parallel-parking their Jeeps or cars wherever they could find a vacant slot; and peanut and balut (cooked, half-hatched duck eggs with embryo—a delicacy to many) vendors vocally advertising their merchandise to the people walking on the sidewalk.

Inspecting a basket half-filled with balut, he asked the vendor, "Are these just cooked?"

"Yes. Feel them. They're still warm."

"How much for two of those?"

"Two pesos and fifty centavos. It would be cheaper to buy five for only five pesos."

"Give me two of those. And don't forget the salt, please."

Marco's transformation from near isolation at the start of classes to having many friends nearly at the end of the school year was an eye opener. No longer a stranger in the community, he felt he belonged. Nonetheless, to his newfound friends in school, Marco was strange in some ways. Not that they cared, or gossiped about a colleague's unconventional ways, particularly a freshman who was still adapting to life in the city. But he was not a mere freshman. Early on in the hallways, classrooms, and conference halls, he displayed the qualities of a budding student leader and a captivating speaker. While his self-confidence continued to flourish, his input and involvement in most extracurricular activities in his department had always been sought.

His peers sifted through his flaws; his "mysterious" ways, if you will. Some of them offered differing views of who they thought he really was and, not surprisingly, aloofness was the leading trait that came to mind. Shyness was a far second. For other friends who'd learned from mutual acquaintances about his pre-college life, however, a theory held that when he was alone, he tended to dwell on a variety of things that were close to his heart: his family in San Antonio, the family farm, his martial arts training, or his next outdoors adventure with his brother and friends during their school breaks. While yet other assessments of him bordered on the preposterous and were ignored, close associates would be amazed to see him every now and then in a vibrant mood, positively interacting with them and enjoying their company.

Despite his oddities, Marco was selfless and cerebral, qualities that often came into play when any classmate needed his assistance with their schoolwork.

Classmates Clara Tavares and Ike Lagasca lived near the beaches of Bauang, a town in the adjoining province of La Union. The two of them were planning an end-of-semester beach party for all the freshmen in their department.

"Which beach resort are we considering?" Ike asked.

"The Sea Breeze in Bauang," Clara said. "They have reasonable rates, and their hall is newly renovated."

"I presume everyone is invited?"

"All freshmen who are interested in joining."

"Not Marco, for God's sake."

"Off course he'll be with us. He's a freshman, and a leader in our department. Where did the negativity come from?" Clara said.

"Marco's kind of weird sometimes. He's a strange fellow whose personality can change very quickly. He can be good-natured one day, but who knows what he'll be the next day. My guess is when we're on the beach, he'll choose to be left alone to sulk under the coconut trees."

"Give him a break, Ike. You're overreacting. He's a sensitive person and can be a deep thinker to a fault, but there's nothing more to that. We all have our quirks. I've known people who act just like him. What's more important is he's upfront and honest, a no-nonsense guy, a leader, a gentleman, and a friend who doesn't hesitate to help others in need."

Marco stayed away from bullies and loudmouths in school, but he would not hesitate to speak out with his displeasure right in their faces if he found them behaving badly. On one occasion, a couple of toughies in school noticed that he was deep in his thoughts while he sat alone on the front lawn. They approached him for no other reason than to browbeat him. They had already made fun of his gangly physique and his occasional peculiar behavior. "What's the matter with you, loner? Seems like your friends got rid of you today," Elmer, one of the two bullies said.

He stared at his heckler, then went on with his business in school, but not before warning them that bullying is never an accepted conduct anywhere. "Enough of it," Marco said. "I've seen and heard of your idiotic behavior, and all I'm asking you is to stay away from me."

The next Saturday afternoon, an altercation was heard at the basketball court behind the auditorium. The two bullies were horse-playing again and when it turned rowdy, a student's foot was hit by a wayward softball bat.

A female student who was passing by told them to stop their improper behavior because it could lead to something serious.

The bullies warned her to mind her own business and not to interfere in their affairs. "We're only having fun and he's not hurt. Just lay off of us."

Marco saw and heard everything. He said in a firm voice, "You guys must stop your stupid activities right now. Act your age and be civil. Your rough acts could seriously injure others."

"This is our business, and who are you to meddle in our affairs or tell us what to do? *Pakialamero ka gaya ni Rita* (You're just as nosy as Rita)," Elmer said, referring to the female student who spoke against their raucous activities.

Marco shot back with defiance and resolve in his eyes, "Whatever you guys do is none of my business, but if it involves aggression, or if it results in injury to others, I'll make it mine."

Elmer and the other bully, Oscar, started to walk toward

Marco, who stood his ground and waited for them to start the fight. He was about to give them a lesson they wouldn't forget. He advised Rita, who stood by to support him, to step away for her safety.

Unlike the two overweight detractors basking in the comfort of their homes, Marco spent a good part of his life outdoors and in the gym. He was slim, strong, and confident in his physical abilities. Owing to his martial arts training, he would avoid fights, but would not back down if he believed that it was justified or when he was attacked, no matter what the consequences.

Mr. Avila, a physical education instructor who saw the hostilities about to turn violent, asked the students to break it up. "If you don't leave the campus right now, I'll call the police," he warned.

"Tandaan mo ito, sa susunod huwag mo kaming pakialaman." The bullies left after Elmer warned Marco against prying in their activities.

The two weeks left of Marco's time in Baguio before the summer school break came and went like a blur. Well, almost. Most of it was spent preparing for and taking the final exams.

After he saw Rita in the hallway talking to a male classmate before entering a classroom to take their final exams, he was frequently in a zone, daydreaming of her. She was resplendent in a dark blue skirt and printed top, wearing a shade of makeup that accentuated her dark, flowing hair and light-brown complexion.

"As I yearn for that new relationship with someone I like and admire, love is in the wings, ready to spring. I don't know what her outlook is on love, or whether she is in a relationship. All I know is my strong desire to pursue that relationship. If I lose, it would bring me to bear on the words of Tennyson: 'Tis better to have loved and lost than never to have loved at all."

After his exam that day, Marco made an effort to find Rita to say goodbye, but that was not to be. He learned that she had left Baguio right after her finals to spend her summer break in her hometown in Calamba, Laguna. The least he could do was to drop her a note, praising her for her brave and noteworthy act when she stood up against the bullies in school. "When classes resume in June, I would hope to meet you again, trusting in an upbeat and peaceful atmosphere," ended his message.

Watching a basketball game at the university auditorium, Marco likened Rita to an errant ball rolling toward a player who dashed to grab it but failing, due to an opposing player who was a tad quicker in the play. Realizing a possible missed opportunity, he took solace in knowing that he would get to see her again in eight weeks.

The bonfire and picnic at the beach turned out to be a huge success. Clara announced during the festivities that the event could pave the way for more beach activities when classes resumed. "There will be more guitar playing, singing of songs like "Dahil Sa Iyo" ("Because of You"), games, and food. Speaking of food, we may add lechon (roast pig) to our menu, to be prepared and roasted right here on the beach. Anything that deviates from the usual brings more fun." Marco, by the way, blended well with his fellow students, especially Ike. He helped Clara and other student leaders in organizing competitive group games that brought laughter to everyone.

He finished reading the final chapter of the memoir Dale Romano had asked him to read. The book recounted the experiences of British author Arthur Miles, who went to Japan to study karate in the early 1960s and progressed to earn a black belt while learning the language and culture. Mr. Takahashi, one of the author's close friends and mentor, who was featured at length in the book, was sent to Manila to teach Shotokan Karate. One of the early black belt graduates was Alvin Arce, now the head instructor of the Japan Karate Association in Baguio.

Marco could hardly wait to rejoin his family as he boarded the first of two connecting buses to San Antonio. The last leg of his trip would be a jeepney ride to his home in the valley.

He looked ahead to enjoying his summer break outdoors with his younger brother, Toby, and their thrill-seeking friends. He hoped to succeed in their forthcoming bid to reach the peak of the dangerous Mount Caasaban.

CHAPTER 2
TALE OF THE DANCING LIGHTS

Ahhh! Saint Elmo's Fire, or Santelmo, as they call it here, is back. The esoteric dancing lights were familiar scenes that he'd encountered perhaps a hundred times or more since childhood. From the lore of the mountains, the legend of the mysterious dancing lights was spun and passed down through generations to rationalize its existence.

The Caraballo Mountain Range, located approximately at the mid-section of the Island of Luzon, links two colossal mountain ranges: the long-stretch Sierra Madre that lies parallel to the northeastern coast, and the Gran Central Cordillera that runs along the central and western spans of the island.

Olin Vega, Marco's father, worked for Northern Consolidated Copper Mine Inc. (NCCMI), a copper, gold, and silver producer. Located on the northern portion of Luzon, the mine was situated in the foothills of the Caraballo Mountains west of the Sierra Madre.

Until two years ago, Olin and Amanda Vega and their teenage sons, Marco and Toby, shared one of the housing facilities the mining company provided. The boys spent their formative years in the mine and their frontier environs.

Amanda's parents, Gil and Marcia Mendoza, bestowed their farm estate to her and her family when the elder couple moved to their second home in San Antonio. After his retirement from the teaching profession, the couple decided to quit farming altogether, to be closer to the hospital, convenience stores, and public transportation.

The Vega family had almost everything they could desire—love, accountability for one's actions, and above all, respect and support for each other. If there was anything more to be asked, it was the maxim that members of a family should sit down at the dinner table together, and often. When Olin began working even harder toward his upcoming company promotion, it didn't take long for Toby to ask his father why they couldn't spend more time together as a family during dinnertime. Olin pointed out that it shouldn't be long before he could spend more time with them. He warned the boys that a family should strive to be together often when possible, but it should not always be viewed as the benchmark of a family's closeness.

Marco and Toby had long outgrown their bunk beds, and wished they had their own spaces. While they knew that their discomfort was only minor, and might even be short-lived, it stimulated their minds to discover their real passion, which was camping outdoors and enjoying the adventures that it provided.

Adept in mountaineering activities, the boys teamed up with their adventurous friends and embarked on a trek to the Caraballo Mountains, camping there for days on end. It was the beginning of a carefree outdoor life that would largely shape their lives, especially Marco's, in the coming years. Although their school breaks were rarely spent at home, Amanda paid no attention to their absences as long as they made good of their promise to stay in school, and mind their responsibilities at home.

When the Vegas moved into their newly inherited, medium-sized farmhouse that included three hectares of developed vegetable farmland, Marco and Toby were ecstatic to find more freedom and breathing space. They had the big valley, the mountains, rivers, canyons, and a cliff all to themselves and their friends when they resumed their outdoor adventures. Likewise, Amanda was pleased to move out from their cottage in the mine to a more spacious house in the farm suburbs of San Antonio.

Saving the best for last, Amanda revealed to the boys that their Lolo Gil bought a handsome young gelding named Aladdin as his moving-in gift for them.

"Your lolo's only request to you both is that you take good care of the horse. You can find Aladdin grazing in the valley next to our farm," she said.

The boys ran to the valley to greet and welcome Aladdin to the family.

When they returned to the house, Marco and Toby were still talking about the horse. They planned on riding the gelding as soon as they were fully settled into their new home. They were overwhelmed with the prospect of teaming up with Aladdin and Gizmo, their German shepherd dog, on a trail ride across the mountains.

"I saw that good-looking bay horse grazing in the valley when we were moving in. I didn't know it was ours," Marco said. "I was tempted to ride it bareback then, but we were too busy moving things from our old home in the mine."

"By the way, there's a saddle and other horseback riding gear in the barn. It must be part of the sale package," Toby advised Marco of his recent find.

"Your lolo told me that the riding gear includes a vintage McClellan saddle in russet brown leather, with matching wooden stirrups and bridle," Amanda said. "He wants you to take good care of them, too."

"Tell lolo we'll take good care of Aladdin and the riding equipment, Mama. And don't forget to thank him and lola for us," Marco said.

"I will, but I'd like you to thank them yourselves when you get the chance to visit them," she said.

"We will, Mama," said Toby. With money left after the renovation and addition of a third bedroom to their house, Olin and Amanda expanded the vegetable farm business her parents left them and decided to invest in livestock—mainly piggery—to complement their farm mix.

Amanda retained the services of Rosie Torres, who had worked at the Gil and Marcia Mendoza Farms for many years. She would now work at the Olin and Amanda Vega Farms.

Olin continued to live inside the mining compound. His home in the farm was forty-eight kilometers away from his home in the mine. Considering the terrain and the condition of the road in bad weather, this distance was too far to travel by public transportation on a daily basis. Carved from the mountainsides, the sole access to the mine was prone to landslides during heavy torrential rains, and much more so during the typhoon season.

He found ways to reach home to help his family with the farm chores during his scheduled days off from work, even when the road became impassable after heavy and continuous downpour.

After they had settled in their farm home in the valley, the brothers put together an association of thrill-seeking young men who loved to hike trails, climb mountains, hunt, and camp in the rugged outdoors during school respites and long holidays. They named their group The Caraballo Hiking Club.

They often camped at their two favorite sites they simply named Campgrounds One and Two.

Most members of the original hiking group eventually relocated to other places or found employment in distant towns. Seven members of the group were still active.

The members of the club hunted birds, trapped wild chicken and other game, caught fishes and frogs, and picked edible mushrooms and other plants for food. Everyone learned how to grill food over the campfire.

The young men discovered that trapping wild chicken could be a very stimulating experience. The best part was that it provided them meat in the mountains when they got lucky. While many other variations in setting up the wild chicken trap existed, Marco had a favorite: light stakes or poles, two meters long, fastened together with strings, were driven vertically into the ground to form a circular compartment two meters in diameter. A net or lattice was tied atop the poles to keep the wild chicken trapped. Rice and corn bait were strewn on the compartment floor. When a wild chicken discovered the grain, it searched for the opening provided at the side of the contraption. Once it entered the one-way door, the wild chicken was trapped inside.

Camping out on the day following his arrival from Baguio, Marco, Toby, their cousin Jonah, and two other hiking club members, Ryan and Pedro, decided to meet the challenge of climbing to the top of Mount Caasaban, in the Caraballo Mountain Range. The peak of the mountain towers at about 1,700 meters—not nearly as high as other mountain peaks on the island, but access to the top was virtually non-existent.

If a trace of a trail were located, it was fragmented, narrow, and dangerously close to the steep hillsides. A misstep could send a mountain climber tumbling down to his or her death at the bottom of the sparsely vegetated precipice. Tough as the ascent was, each of them was also weighed down by at least thirty kilograms of supplies and camping equipment. Seasonal expectations this time of the year included inclement weather characterized by heavy rain, thunder, lightning, fog, and gusty winds, which would intensify the risk in reaching the top.

After a day and a half of arduous climbing, Marco, the leader of the group, warned, "We're making progress getting to the top of the mountain, but more work remains. We're nowhere near the peak, but I'd say we've passed the midway point. We must start looking for a place to camp and resume the climb at daybreak. Heavy rain and strong winds appear to be bearing down on our location, and I'm afraid it can batter us any moment now."

Weighing their two options, whether to continue their ascent or set up camp, the climbers chose the latter. They would have to look for a suitable campsite, pitch tents, and let the impending high winds and rainstorm run their courses before they continued their climb the next day.

As expected, a heavy torrential downpour accompanied by winds with gusts beat down on the mountains and valleys below. Not to be outdone, lightning and thunder flicked and rumbled in quick succession across the rugged terrain. Everyone tried to keep himself safe and dry by hunkering close to the trees with thick foliage. As the downpour intensified and the dark clouds obscured the sun, visibility took a turn for the worse.

"Thunderstorms usually last for thirty minutes or maybe a little longer," Marco said. "Although they have short durations, they can be quite intense and getting caught in them, as we are now, can be a real challenge. Let's stay together and be safe. The bad weather will pass and we hope, the electrical storm, too."

As darkness started to creep in and the fog and rain affected visibility, there was no doubt in their minds that the situation could turn for the worse after sunset. The mountain climbers were faced with the prospect of not finding a suitable campsite for the night.

Marco volunteered to find one while there was still light.

The rain diminished as fast as it had begun, but not before the area was flooded with debris everywhere. It seemed like tens of thousands of buckets of water were dumped from the skies over a short period of time, causing flashfloods that cascaded down the hillsides.

Scanning the foothills of Mount Caasaban across the terraced rice fields, Marco made a sweeping glance at the lights that lit the homes far down the valley. Sparsely arrayed, the quaint illuminations drew his attention.

But what soon captured his interest were lights of a different nature that suddenly emerged from the expansive space above the farmed river valley. Once again, he stood in awe and gazed at the very mysterious spectacle he had seen many times before; an organized congregation of flickering, dancing lights that moved swiftly in unison across short distances, often shuttling back close to the same spot from which they originated. The dancing lights had been observed to linger no longer than one second in one location. They continued to dart and move around in one bunch, often splitting into several bunches as they were set in motion anew, only to flit away and die as others were born. Known to be constantly changing locations, the usually bluish-white dancing lights didn't necessarily conform to certain patterns of motion, but rather followed a random and elaborate displacement process. The displays were fleeting— similar to but considerably speedier and less dazzling than the pyrotechnics exhibits seen in many urban celebrations.

"Ahh! Saint Elmo's Fire, or Santelmo as it is called here,

is back," Marco observed. It was a familiar scene that he'd encountered perhaps a hundred times or more throughout his childhood. He often noted that the dancing lights were short-lived—their lifespan measured in minutes—and their evening or night apparitions were frequent. The lights usually appeared at the tail ends of heavy rain and thunderstorms. They were known to shape up and reveal their presence during dry weather as well.

From the lore of the mountains, the favorite legend of the dancing lights was spun and passed down through generations. It professes that the esoteric lights embody the spirit of Tobias Sanvictores, who had encountered a bizarre misfortune while hiking from his work to his home in the village.

Employed by the government, Tobias was a caminero, or road maintenance worker. Each day throughout the workweek he hiked the rugged trail from his home to his workplace and back again, a total distance of twenty-five kilometers. A happy and spry fifty-year-old man, he more than met the physical requirements of his daily regimen. If he had one obvious flaw it was his habit of downing a few swigs of his favorite Tanduay rum in the town's sari-sari (convenience) store; not to get intoxicated, but to imbibe just the right quantity to lift his body and spirit for his long walk home. If he heard disparaging remarks about his drinking habit, he had a well-thought reply that he would use even when it was raining, "It'll wash down the dirt accumulated in my throat after a hard day's work on that dusty span."

During a typical night's hike to his home in the village, he would descend the trail that runs through a gurgling brook, hop onto the double-logged bridge to reach the opposite bank, and continue his pace homeward.

The intersection of the double-logged bridge and the brook were lushly vegetated with ferns, brushes, and old-growth trees that were covered with mosses and vines. It was dark under the canopy, even during a full moon or when the stars were lighting up the sky. The one conspicuous thing passersby would notice there at night was the peculiar outline of the drooping branches being weighed down by the clinging vines.

Crossing the brook had been a routine matter to him until he began to hear strange sounds at night. Even during breezeless nights, he would hear vigorous rustling of leaves that would corroborate the stories of other spooked passersby.

What's more, the cacophonous sounds of the birds and insects, combined with that of the gurgling brook, was just as unnerving.

One Friday evening after work, Tobias went to his usual watering hole with his friend and co-worker, Pacifico.

He had one drink too many, but was confident that he could manage to walk home on his own. He knew the route like the back of his hand. He revealed to his friend the dark secrets around the brook that he could no longer keep to himself. "I am quite terrified every time I hear the creepy sounds I simply can't explain. I have no other way to get home since there's no detour, and it's not possible to cut a different route on that rugged terrain."

"Frogs, crickets, and certain birds produce strange sounds; we both know that," Pacifico said.

"I'm positive that the noises I've been hearing for many nights were not given off by animals and insects we see and hear in our world. As I recall, the sounds that reached my ears were moans and garbled cries that seemed to be coming from a burdened spirit that moved into the brook area and made it his abode," Tobias said. "I dared not point my flashlight directly at the trees and vines above for fear of retribution by the specter if he finds that I have discovered his presence in the area."

"You can sleep in my home tonight," Pacifico offered. "We're off work tomorrow. I'm sure you'll feel better when you walk home in the morning."

Tobias politely declined the invitation. He always made it a point to be home every night, tipsy or sober. Not even a supernatural presence along his route could stop him.

"Goodnight my good friend … and goodbye," Tobias said, both hands tightly clasping Pacifico's right hand. "Thanks for listening to my troubles."

Once more, he hiked the trail to his home in the village as he had for many years. It was his final hike home. He was never seen nor heard from again.

To his dying day, Pacifico held fast to his conviction that his good friend, Tobias, devised the dancing lights and took its form, wandering through the hills and valleys, mountains and canyons, rivers and lakes and all the seas and oceans, in expectation that one day someone would discover his remains and bring them to their final resting place.

The dancing lights were gone.

And the legend lives on.

When Marco crossed a drainage gulch overflowing with water and silt, his mind still occupied by the legend of the dancing lights and the spectacle he had just witnessed, he lost his balance and slipped. He was carried down by the swift current.

It was a long slide down the steep and slippery gulch into a deep pool at the bottom of the spillway. Finding himself waist-deep in water and mud, he could hardly move. His lower body was mired in a pasty sludge.

He shouted at the top of his voice for help a few times, but no one could hear him. He was too far down the ravine. The other climbers could not hear his voice over the noise of water rushing down the hillsides.

A half-hour passed. Toby began to wonder about Marco.

"Where did he go? Shouldn't he be back by now?"

Jonah volunteered to find out why Marco wasn't back yet. Walking across the slippery slopes, it didn't take long before he saw footprints on the water-soaked ground.

"No doubt these are his shoe prints. They're still fresh."

He followed the foot marks until he came across a large volume of water rushing down, like a small waterfall, into the steep drainage gulch.

"Marco's footprints ended where the waterfall started," Jonah whispered his observation.

Over the pervading noise coming from every direction he called out Marco's name loudly, but there was no answer. He screamed at the top of his voice. Still, there was no answer.

Jonah realized the danger that the small waterfall presented. It was muddy and slippery all around, and he feared that he could slip and lose his footing and be carried down to the bottom of the steep hillside by the swift current.

That's a long drop to the pit below.

Then, he heard a faint sound coming from the bottom of the ravine. He shouted Marco's name again and heard the same muffled sound.

It struck Jonah that something had gone terribly wrong. He felt cold sweat over his body and was gasping for breath. He feared for Marco's life, realizing that the muffled sounds were his. Who else but Marco would be down there?

Oh my God! He was probably screaming for help. He could have slipped and got swept down by the swift current. I would go down there to help him right now, but I need a piece of rope to hold onto for support. "Hang in there, Marco! Help's coming!" he shouted again, hoping that Marco would hear him.

He went back to inform the party that Marco needed help,

fast. He slung a rope over his shoulder and led Toby and the other climbers to the shortest pathway to reach him.

Marco, meanwhile, removed his belt and shirt and tied them together to fashion a rope to extricate himself from the muddy water. He saw a tree stump above that he tried to lasso to lift himself out of the trap.

He found that the makeshift rope was a bit short for the purpose he had in mind. "If I had more shirts on my back …" he said, touching his back. "Hey, I can use my undershirt!"

Jonah pointed out to Toby where the muffled screams had come from. They skirted around the small waterfall that had since weakened after the flash downpour died down. They scaled the slope using a different path that seemed less slippery. Toby and Jonah tied one end of the rope to a tree and, grasping it for support, went down the steep and rain-saturated hillside. Their two hiking buddies stayed at the top end of the rope to pull them up if necessary. When Toby and Jonah reached the bottom, they were surprised to see the shirtless Marco, muddied up to his waist, and standing next to the tree stump that he'd used to pull himself out of the mire.

Jonah visualized the entire series of events that began with Marco's hard slide down in an upright position and ended when his lower extremities were swallowed by the pool of mud at the bottom of the pit. What he couldn't figure out was how Marco was able to drag himself out of the sticky sludge.

Toby assumed that Marco had learned his lesson and would henceforth be wary when crossing swift water currents on the hillsides during flashfloods.

With their flashlights, the climbers attempted to look for spring water to wash themselves and clean their soiled clothes but decided against it when they became aware of the danger of falling.

"We filled our canteens with rainwater at the height of the

thunderstorm," Marco said. "That's all the water we'll need till morning."

"You'll need more water to wash the dirt from your body. We'll share some of the water in our canteens with you," Toby said.

The mountain climbers set up their camp—albeit in a bad location. They dried their wet and muddy clothes by the fire. They warmed their food and ate a late supper.

The next day they resumed their quest to set foot on the peak of the mountain. After more than five hours of a punishing climb, they found themselves standing on the pinnacle of the grand and lofty Mount Caasaban.

CHAPTER 3

THE MAYOR'S GAMBIT

I truly believe that if we can't coexist with them, we can do
our part to protect and help them exist away from us.

TWO YEARS EARLIER

The eagles' home range, deep in the lush rainforest of the northern Sierra Madre Mountains, was in turmoil at that moment. The faunal inhabitants of the active forest canopy scrambled to safety, many of them diving to the safer understory.

Birds of various species, including a pair of owls and other birds of prey, sensed the impending danger as they darted in every direction to escape from the still unseen peril that was coming their way. Feathers were afloat everywhere, setting that part of the wilderness in utmost disarray.

Shrieking, gliding, swerving, and flapping their enormous wings, a pair of huge and ferocious monkey-eating eagles appeared out of nowhere under the thick jungle cover pierced by blinding slivers of sunlight. Ignoring smaller prey in their sights, the winged predators navigated through the maze of trees and vines commingled with other forest growth in the hunt of a more inviting game they'd caught sight of outside the densely wooded area.

One of the giant eagles landed on a tree in the clearing. A bunch of monkeys playing on the tree across became restive at the sight of the huge predator nearby. Meanwhile, with doggedness and hustle, the equally menacing mate swooped down like an arrow and snatched a monkey from its perch.

The brazen eagles, one of them grasping its prey, flew back to their nest. Soon after, orderly co-existence of the occupants of the rainforest prevailed once more.

In the absence of other fierce predators in the jungle— such as tree-climbing big cats and other large predatory birds not endemic to the islands—this pair of eagles continued to enhance their newly acquired physical stature and strength, prevailing over other predators in upholding their superior position in the food chain.

Monkey-eating eagles hunt for food as needed. They mate when it is the right time—there is no observed breeding cycle— and produce an average of one fledgling every other year.

One day, the giant predators crossed their boundaries and ventured into populated frontier towns within soaring distance from their home range. The eagles seemed to have grown tired of hunting smaller prey in their territory and began attacking domestic animals in those towns. Other reasons for this behavior were worth looking into, but this one might explain why the eagles pushed their envelope.

One community often beset by the giant eagles was the town of Santa Teresa, a sprawling agricultural community containing large areas of farmed land. The town is nestled in the foothills of Mount Amador, which is part of the Sierra Madre Mountain Range.

The developed areas are sufficiently irrigated, and as grain production continued to expand, the potential of becoming a major producer of rice and corn in the region was in the realm of possibility.

Santa Teresa is also home to a number of small livestock farms: poultry, piggery, cattle, some goats, and sheep.

The frontier town was erstwhile calm until the fearsome eagles began to terrorize the farmers by attacking and whisking off their livestock. A pig, a pair of goats, several small dogs, two gamecocks, a sheep, and many other domestic animals had disappeared; some of the attacks were witnessed, others were alleged.

This unfortunate turn of events brought about paranoia, anger, and restlessness amongst the town's residents.

The winged predators became an increasingly troubling thought for most residents of the community. Town Mayor Gene Salvador, having obtained a quiet nod from the municipal council, took the problem directly to the grassroots level and convened a meeting with the residents. The agenda: What shall we do with the eagles?

The assembly was composed of more than ninety residents. Half of them stood in the aisles and in the back of the hall, far outnumbering the fifty seats available in the school building for town meetings.

Mayor Gene, as he was fondly called by his constituents, was aware that the predators fell in disfavor with the population, especially the livestock farmers. He was told that the resentment spread into the neighboring towns as well. He was prepared to meet with the town residents to assuage them of their fears and concerns about the predators.

Gene had long sought for a solution to the problem. Of late, he believed that he had contrived a scheme he hoped the town residents would approve and support.

The plan, though radical and untried, was an option he thought may be worthy of favorable consideration, and was eager to present it to the public during the course of the meeting.

The eagles' attacks would be rehashed during the early part of the meeting to provide the public with some insight regarding the eagles' infractions that incited the ire of the livestock farmers. Residents who were not in town during the predators' attacks would benefit from the briefing.

Witnesses to the attacks were called upon to brief the town residents of their experiences.

Johnny Saldana, the first witness, was called upon to relate his experience with the predators. He informed the gathered folks that he saw a huge bird of prey, an eagle, lunging at a goat that was grazing at a neighbor's fenced property. Clutching its prey with its massive talons, the eagle flew westward toward the thickly forested area. He followed its flight path as far as his eyes could see, but he found it impossible to determine where the predator's flight terminated. It may have landed at some point to rest en route to its destination, or it could have soared directly to its nest while clutching its prey.

He used a field compass and a map of the area to plot the direction of flight the eagle followed from his neighbor's property to the rainforest area. He tied the flight path to natural landmarks for reference.

Vice Mayor Victor Young told the crowd that he saw a huge eagle, the biggest he had ever seen, swoop down and carry off a young goat grazing inside a fenced pasture near his farm. "I didn't take the stand tonight to repeat what you've seen or heard before. Rather, I'm here to tell you that in my brief glances of the attack, I saw an eagle of very large proportions, bigger than any winged predator I've previously seen. I swear that I saw a giant monkey-eating eagle—and I'm not alluding to the world of fantasy or fairy tales. I think that left to hunt in the rainforest by themselves without having to contend with worthy competitors for food, they naturally grew huge. It's just unfortunate that they went beyond their bounds and attacked and carried off some of our domestic livestock."

He recalled that the eagles' hostile actions began more than two years ago and to his surprise, there was no proposal to alleviate the festering problem. "Perhaps the affected townsfolk decided to bear it without complaining, assuming that the incidents were random and would not recur," he said. "I accept part of the blame as a town official."

Three other witnesses were called upon to speak about their experiences with the aggressive eagles. They had similar accounts to share with the assembled folks. Each one narrated his tale of a pair of overgrown eagles, one slightly bigger than the other, the strength and ferocity of which they had never seen nor heard of before.

Many had observed, at one time or another, the eagle mates soaring in the sky or perched on a high bough near the edge of town, waiting to dive and attack prey, domestic or wild. The predators had been hunting separately or jointly in Santa Teresa and other neighboring communities.

"One of the predators," the last speaker said, "easily carried its prey off to their nesting site, presumed to be inside the Santa Magdalena rainforest."

A woman with a child strode to the rostrum and advised those with small children to be extra careful, and not to let the toddlers walk or play outside their house unattended. "Children can be very vulnerable to the predators," she warned, as she made eye contact with parents who had young children of their own.

"What shall we do with the eagles?" Mayor Gene asked the assembly.

His question triggered off a tumultuous reaction from the crowd. Loud and emphatic voices were heard from some of the townsfolk suggesting that somebody ought to shoot the big birds with air guns or low-caliber rifles. Others suggested the use of more powerful shotguns or high-caliber rifles.

"Use anything from guns to poison darts but kill them all!

Blast them to pieces if you can!" shouted an angry man whose two tethered champion gamecocks had disappeared from his backyard.

The mayor tried to calm down the madding crowd, politely "shushing" them and gesturing that they must control their emotions and listen to what he had to say.

"Ladies and gentlemen, if we work together, we can put an end to these unfortunate events. The eagles seem very aggressive and unstoppable, but I can assure you that we can do something about it. That's what this meeting is about. Please calm down and listen carefully," he said. "I would strongly suggest not killing the eagles but driving them off to the far reaches of the island where they can reestablish their territory and seek new hunting ranges."

A protest started to brew inside the hall. Several owners of livestock that had gone missing or were seen to have been attacked and whisked away by the eagles objected to the mild redress suggested by Mayor Gene.

Frank, whose champion gamecocks went missing, said, "Are you suggesting, Mr. Mayor, that the eagles be spared their lives and merely driven away from their home territory? I say that's too mild a punishment for them."

"That's what I said, and that's what I'd propose. It's an idea that I thought might be worth presenting to the participants of this meeting for approval at some point during our meeting tonight," Gene said. "Short of killing them, can anyone share with us what he or she thinks is more severe than forcing them out of the habitat they've known as home since they were fledglings?"

No one in the hall offered a response to Gene's question. Pleased with the public's non-committal stance, he could smell his impending triumph on the matter.

Still, there was the issue of convincing the town residents

that forcing the predators out of their home territory, unharmed, was the right thing to do.

"It was the consensus among the speakers tonight that the eagles are nested in the thickly forested area west of Santa Teresa. We must find their nest to drive them off. It could be a difficult task, but I believe it's doable," Gene said.

He suggested that the search be concentrated in the Santa Magdalena rainforest, taking into consideration the eagle's flight heading and the reference points Johnny plotted on his map.

"Searching for the eagles' nest may take several days to carry out, given the vast area of wilderness that we must scour to find it," he said, pausing to light a cigarette.

As he collected his thoughts and waited for the people to calm down, Gene directed the assembly to prepare to bring the matter to a vote. "Those who are in favor of driving the eagles away from Santa Teresa, unharmed, please raise your right hands. Not to be harmed, I repeat."

The referendum was quickly decided. The majority of the assembly concurred with Gene's proposal.

"We are headed in the right direction. I'm very pleased with the mandate," he said. "Thank you all very much. Now we can proceed to the next phase of the meeting—the execution of the plan that I am anxious to present when we reconvene after a fifteen-minute break."

The mayor resumed the meeting by presenting his plan to use firearms to drive the eagles away. Before going into the details of the plan, he asked for volunteers to determine if there were enough men willing and able to do the job.

"Volunteers must be active hunters who either own or have access to hunting rifles, and have used them in the past. They must be capable of carrying out a special task that entails the search of the eagles' nest in order to drive them away from the Santa Magdalena rainforest," he said. "No one can predict where the eagles will end up. I'll keep my fingers crossed until I'm told that they have dispersed to the pristine wilderness of the northeast Sierra Madre Mountains."

Five men promptly raised their hands. The sixth person raised his hand after his brother offered to loan him his hunting rifle. The volunteer's own rifle needed repairs and replacement of certain parts.

Mayor Gene thanked the hunters for volunteering to take on the difficult task. He praised them for their service to the community, and assured them that their efforts would be inscribed in the records of their town's history.

"Most of us are aware that this undertaking is not by any means a walk in the park. Hunters and hikers are aware of the hazards that could befall them in the woods. The risks include exposure to poisonous arthropods and reptiles, bloodsucking leeches, mosquitoes that could spread malaria or dengue fever, toxic plants, and other disease-causing organisms. There could be other hazards currently unknown," he said.

When a town resident asked how long it might take the hunters to finish the task, Gene volunteered a guess of anywhere from three to seven days. "More importantly, we hope that they can accomplish the job in just one trip to the wilderness," he said.

"Now, to continue with the presentation of the plan I devised not long ago; when the nest is found, fire at the eagles at will but only to scare—not to kill. Always aim your firearms at least half a meter away from them. When shooting at the direction of the elevated nest, watch the trajectory of your bullets, and make sure the slugs fall into unpopulated areas. Let me remind you of the presence of indigenous tribes in that area. They are seldom seen but be aware of their presence there.

Be extra careful," he implored.

"If the plan fails, what's the next option?" a skeptical town resident asked.

"We'll meet here again to decide how to take out those menacing predators. I'm sure there are other ways to get rid of them, but killing the eagles should be our last recourse," the mayor said.

The town's top executive adjourned the public meeting, but asked his six volunteers and the vice mayor to stay for a few more minutes to work out some details of the project.

For safety reasons, Gene suggested that the volunteers should look for the eagles' nest in groups of two and make their search during daylight hours only.

He told Victor Young and the six volunteers that the idea of driving the eagles away and sparing their lives was his, and he would accept full responsibility if anything went awry.

Though he was convinced that his scheme would bring immediate positive results, he warned them that they must navigate through uncharted territory in the days ahead.

He underscored the need for the volunteers' full support if success could be expected.

The team members collectively vowed to implement the plan to the utmost of their abilities.

Again, the mayor reiterated the need to avoid, under any circumstances, bodily harm upon the eagles. He reminded them that the predators were increasingly disappearing from their niches and were quickly declining in numbers from anywhere they are found in the country. This modest effort could be a last-ditch attempt to protect them and help them survive.

"Though many residents of Santa Teresa, along with those of neighboring communities, have shown disdain of the eagles—and justifiably so—others value them for what they are; a unique species of raptors found only on our islands. They are faced with many adversities that threaten their very existence. They're worth saving as far as I'm concerned, and I know that you'll all agree with me. I truly believe that if we can't coexist with them, we can do our part to protect and help them exist apart from us," Gene said.

CHAPTER 4
BANISHED TO
THE NORTH EAST?

*The winged predators will find a new sanctuary far
beyond our horizons and well inside the unspoiled
northeastern Sierra Madre Rainforest. This will help
enhance their survival and that of their species.*

The six volunteers were avid outdoorsmen who shared
similar experiences and pursuits. As decided by the
townspeople of Santa Teresa, they embarked on an all-
out search of the eagles for the purpose of driving them out of
their home territory.

These men were all seasoned hunters who could hold their
own in the wilderness. With the exception of Cicero, whose
experience teaching literature in high school was followed by
working in construction as a senior drafter, farming had always
been their primary means of livelihood.

The volunteers were passionate about hunting and fishing
and simply straying outdoors at every chance of escape that
their occupations allowed.

The beginning of their journey to the eagles' territory was
spent in a hired Jeep that took them tens of kilometers on a
narrow and winding road until they reached a trail that forked
from the road. They switched to footwork on that trail and
expected to continue hiking the rest of the way.

During the second phase of their trip, they crossed corn fields and rice paddies until they reached the bank of a river that runs through the farmland. They followed the river's edge upstream for several kilometers until they reached their pre-selected staging point. The ultimate and most difficult phase of their journey began with an eastward ascent toward the forested area, presumed to be the eagles' home range.

The six hunters split into three two-member teams of Ricky and Mario, Freddie and Danny, and Cicero and Tony.

As each team was expected to operate independently until the predators' nest was located, communication between the teams was limited to the discharge of their low caliber sidearms. When there was a need to alert or relay information to the other teams, the members agreed to follow a pre-determined code, to wit: A single discharge from a side firearm would mean everything is in accordance to plans, carry on; two discharges would mean we need your help immediately; three discharges would mean the eagles' nest had been located. The two other teams must reconvene immediately with the team that found the eagles' nest. Then they would all commence to fire their rifles in order to drive the eagles away.

Each team fanned out and ascended the hills using separate paths for broad coverage. Freddie and Danny ascended the mountain by way of an old trail they followed after they left the riverbank staging point. Climbing the steep slopes was tough, but it was many times as difficult to rise to the top of the badly eroded gullies.

The two other teams blazed new trails but were not too far behind the leading team.

Standing atop the ridge after the torturous climb, the pace-setting duo trimmed back their energies as they began to tread on moderate terrain.

They had lost the old trail they'd followed uphill for many

kilometers.

"I'm not too concerned about losing the old trail. We'll use our map and compass to navigate the rest of the way," Danny said.

"Let's rest while we eat our lunch here," Freddie said, pulling out his lunch from his duffel bag.

"Why don't we eat on the flat clearing under that big tree? It's closer to the spring water and we can refill our canteens there," Danny said.

Grabbing their duffel bags and rifles to resume their journey, thunder rumbled amid the crackle of lightning. Big drops of rain pelted down soon after. They quickly slipped on their pullover raincoats and took shelter under the tree.

"The rain makes the ground slushy. Let's wait for the storm to weaken before we move on," Danny said, observing the dark rain clouds that had blocked the sun.

"Damn this rain," Freddie said, decrying the intense afternoon soaker. "We are losing precious time on account of this downpour."

"We live in a tropical zone," Danny told his partner. "Keep in mind that abundance of rain is what we can expect seven to eight months of the year."

"I realize that. There's nothing we can do about it."

Enduring the intermittent rain showers, occasional gusty winds, and muddy ground, they continued to make headway in their push to reach the outskirts of the forest before dark.

Just as the rain stopped and the sky cleared a bit, the pair saw the spectacular southwestern ridge of the vast wilderness in the distance.

"The rainforest scenery looks very much alive and soothing to the eyes. Check out the green vegetation and the trees that appear untouched," Danny, who had not been to the rainforest for several years, said.

"It's a welcome sight after plodding through fog and mud," Freddie agreed.

Approximating the time it would take them to reach the target camp area from their current location, Danny said, "While we are still far off, we could reach the edge of the rainforest and camp there before nightfall."

The shadows were deepening when the pair reached their planned camp site en route to the eagles' territory.

They set up camp on a level surface next to the trees and built a fire between their tents. The duo brewed coffee over the crackling fire and heated their home-prepared, ready-to-eat food. Both retired for the night feeling quite exhausted.

They woke at daybreak, fresh and energized to face another grueling day in the forest. The rough terrain hike the day before left no lasting effect on them.

After eating a hearty breakfast, they doused their campfire and planned the day's activity. They reviewed their map and rechecked their current position to make sure they were on track in their search, taking into consideration the previously established flight path obtained from Johnny Saldana's map.

"Time to find out how the other teams are doing. I'll send them a message," Danny said; he aimed his .22 revolver skyward and fired.

The men from the other teams quickly responded with single discharges from their handguns. The shots seemed to have originated from different locations, although both men agreed that they were fired from the same slopes that they'd climbed the day before.

"Very good!" Danny exclaimed, and pointed at the approximate locations the shots came from. "It's good to know that the other teams are doing as well as can be expected."

"The men on the slopes must be ascending the steep hillsides even as we speak, having camped there the previous night. It's apparent that they have spent extra time blazing new trails to reach the slopes," Freddie said.

Danny speculated that the other teams were still hours away from reaching the edge of the jungle. No matter. The job at hand could take a few days or longer to carry out. The other volunteers could certainly catch up and help them track down the eagles using alternate routes to the deeper parts of the jungle.

As they entered the narrow pathways between the trunks of the broad-leaved dipterocarp trees and the lush ferns and rhododendrons, the team navigated their way, pushing into the lush growth of trees and a host of other vegetation.

They wore thick, knee-high socks and appropriate clothing to protect themselves from leeches, mosquitoes, and other annoying and potentially deadly denizens of the jungle.

Encountering poisonous snakes was not their biggest worry, although they were aware of a presence and would exercise extreme caution at all times. "Bothersome insects and worms deserve more attention than reptiles," Danny said. "Leeches are blood-sucking worms and not known to carry disease-causing organisms. They could cause irritation if they stick to the skin with their tiny suction cups and are difficult to scrape off until they are fully engorged in blood."

Freddie and Danny took their position in the rainforest, carefully watching their surroundings and listening for signs of the dreaded pair of giant eagles. They expected to hear the eagles' shrill whistles and the periodic flapping of wings under the rainforest canopy. They awaited the high-pitched squeals of a hungry eaglet in a nest high above the ground.

The two other teams reached the perimeter of the rainforest

from different routes. They pushed deeper into the dense jungle, hoping to find the eagles' nest in a short time. The three teams were inside the rainforest for more than three days watching and listening for signs of the eagles. They camped in the jungle with no communication; each team not knowing what the other teams had learned about their quarry. Each of the men knew what was expected of him to accomplish the task.

Ricky and Mario estimated that the trees reached heights up to twenty meters or more. The thick canopy stood lower than the tallest trees. Provided with the knowledge that the eagles would likely build their nest on the crowns of tall trees, they watched the emergent ones with thick and sturdy crowns.

Using basic sign language, the men continued to patrol the rainforest quietly, with nary a word uttered. They kept watch for any unusual movement of any occupant of the forest.

On the fourth day of their search, Freddie and Danny were startled by a loud whir of wings followed by raucous agitation of the inhabitants of the jungle.

Every potential eagle's prey, as well as non-prey flew, climbed, or dove in every direction in order to keep out of the way of two giant eagles gliding and flapping between trees, one clutching a lifeless monkey in its claws.

The team was extremely excited to discover the eagles' territory at last.

They ran toward the source of the noise and had a quick glimpse of the brown and white eagles as they found their way between the trees below the canopy. They lost sight of the winged predators for a moment, but were able to track them down as they landed atop a tall, broad-leaved tree.

The men were quick to seek higher ground without losing sight of the top of the tree. From the elevated earthen platform where they stood, the pair watched the three predators perched on the huge nest resting on the crown of the tree.

The volunteers had tracked the eagles for almost four days, enduring relentless afternoon rain, mud, and cold nights. They also fought mosquitoes, leeches, and bugs.

Making sure that all the safety protocols were observed, Freddie and Danny positioned themselves to fire their rifles in the direction of the nest, but not aiming directly at the hungry birds that could be seen tearing their lifeless prey apart.

"We're still not seen by the giant eagles. Let's be careful and shoot accurately," Freddie reminded Danny.

Danny fired three shots in the air with the gun muzzle pointed high above the nest.

The other teams understood what the three volleys meant; the eagles' nest was found. They quickly sprinted toward the sound of gunfire.

After a short pause, Danny and Freddie commenced firing, deliberately missing the nest. They were no longer firing their rifles to send a message to the other teams; the duo were discharging their guns to drive the eagles out of their nest.

Delighted to jump into the fray, the two other teams reached the eagles' territory with their rifles pointed upward and ready for action.

After exchanging hushed greetings with the other team members, they began to fire their rifles as fast as they could be reloaded. Two to four rifles were fired simultaneously.

The eagles' territory looked like a firing range as smoke and the smell of gunpowder filled the air.

"Hold your fire! Hold your fire!" shouted Danny. He signaled the other men to lay their rifles aside and observe the reaction of the eagles.

The volunteers saw a fledgling fly from the nest to other parts of the jungle. The men were moved by the scene, knowing that the eaglet would have to find a new home and survive on its own. They hoped that the fledgling would find ample prey to hunt in the wild. Without other aggressive predators to compete for the available food there, it should hold its own, find a mate when it matured in a few years, and continue its bloodline.

The adult eagles were still atop their nest.

On cue, the volunteers resumed firing their rifles, hoping that they would be able to drive the predators away before they ran out of bullets. They aimed closer to the nest. Some bullets broke twigs that were holding the nest in place.

When one of the giant eagles flew out of the nest, its right wing was grazed by a bullet. Feathers flew and floated everywhere while the predator continued to fly away, its mate following close behind.

"Stop firing!" Danny, the self-appointed leader of the group, shouted again amid the staccato of ear-piercing gunfire echoing in the forest. "The eagles are gone, with our anticipation that they will never return to this rainforest for their own good. Let's hope they find another home in a similar forest away from us."

Cicero, who was more knowledgeable of monkey-eating eagles than anyone else in the group, suggested that they must destroy the eagles' nest to minimize the chances of their return to the same nesting area. "Pairs of eagles almost always go back to their old nests after they have fledged and are ready to breed again, even if they have built new nests elsewhere. If the pair were to return and find their nest gone, chances are they would leave permanently and seek other nesting territories. Hopefully it will be in the Sierra Madre wilderness," he said.

Everyone listened and took heed of his suggestion.

They shot at and totally destroyed the huge eagles' nest, decimating the crown of the tree in the process.

The men were hopeful to be back to hunt in the Santa

Magdalena Rainforest at some point, but they couldn't stand the thought of repeating this particular mission.

"Let us hope that the fledgling who just got separated from its parents was hatched a year ago or around that time. If it was hatched much later, it would be too young to hunt on its own," Cicero said. "It has been observed that quite a number of young eagles do not reach maturity for certain reasons. I suppose one of those reasons could be their early separation from their parents before they can fend for themselves. The recently detached eaglet, if mature enough to hunt, may have a good chance of survival given the right environment, and the light competition for the available food in these rainforests."

"Let's leave a lasting memento in this former home of the giant eagles so that other outdoorsmen may learn of their existence and struggles here," Danny said.

Freddie carved a sign on the trunk of the huge tree that once supported the huge nest. It read:

THE GREAT GIANT EAGLES
LIVED AND HUNTED HERE - Until April 1970

Since the plan's inception during the town meeting, the majority of the six volunteers didn't buy Mayor Gene's perceived notion that certain animals in the wild, including the eagles, would scuttle their home territories and disperse when subjected to a powerful stimulus such as heavy gunfire.

Still, they supported the scheme, and felt that the gambit was well worth the shot. It seemed the only option left for them. Killing or maiming the eagles would be totally unacceptable.

The volunteers' four-day foray in the wilderness culminated in their victory. Would it benefit Santa Teresa and other neighboring communities? A positive outcome at this point could be anticipated.

The men parlayed their success into hope and expectation that those affected in livestock farming in all communities could resume their regular activities without fear of loss of property—thus increasing the likelihood that the eagles' survival would be much enhanced.

Feeling giddy in the ensuing excitement, they sat on the forest floor to savor their victory. Looking back at the day's events, however, the men were overwhelmed by guilt and shame.

"What have we done to the eagles?" Danny exclaimed. Like Cicero and the rest of the volunteers, he began to feel remorse after watching the big birds fly away hurriedly to an unknown location, leaving the nesting place they'd known as home for many years. One eagle was accidentally grazed by a bullet during the fracas, and no one knew exactly where it was hit or how bad the injury was. And to top it all, the eaglet was forced into an untimely emancipation.

Despite the chaos the predators raised in the community not long ago, many residents held the giant birds in high esteem.

It dawned on the hunters that eagles are a special breed of predators. Pound for pound, they are the best hunters in the skies, in the rainforests, and on the ground. Their flying skills are almost beyond comparison. They are fierce and unrelenting hunters. Their size, wingspan, and strength are unrivaled among other winged predators, inciting both fear and respect from the people of Santa Teresa and neighboring communities.

The six hunters took one last look at the destroyed crown of the tree that once held the huge nest of the winged predators.

"May the eagles find peaceful and productive existence in the jungles of the northeast, and may their species continue to survive and thrive," Danny said.

Peace and quiet prevailed once more in the wilderness, save for the harsh cacophony generated by the birds, crickets, frogs, and a host of other creatures present in the jungle.

Sadly trudging on the forest floor, the hunters packed their guns, supplies, and camping equipment in preparation for their trip out of the woods.

Darkness was creeping in when the men reached the outskirts of the forest. The "mission-completed" feeling tucked under their belts, the men settled down and set up their camp for the night.

"We should be on our way home after breakfast in the morning," Cicero said.

That evening, the hunters were listless as they sought the warmth and comfort of the campfire. Missing were the vigor and laughter they'd brought with them when they began their voluntary task. The giant eagles seemed to have cast a dark pall upon them, each one consumed by thoughts of the big birds they brutally drove away, including the hapless fledgling.

They'd accomplished what they were asked to do, and then some. They pushed nature's boundaries by not leaving the flying predators to live their role in the food chain process. By the same token, they helped save their winged "friends" from harm or death in the hands of those who occupied the highest echelon in the food chain—men.

The volunteers were proud to have served their community.

It appeared that no matter how extreme or untried the plan looked at the time, it could prove to be a resounding success once the predators moved permanently from the Santa Magdalena Rainforest to the uninhabited wilderness of the northeast.

Mayor Gene thanked all those who were involved with the task of banishing the eagles and expressed his hope that: "The winged predators will find a new sanctuary far beyond our horizons and well inside the unspoiled northeastern Sierra Madre Rainforest. This will help enhance their survival and that of their species."

CHAPTER 5
MYSTERIOUS VISIT

*How strange it is to see this magnificent, winged predator
in these mountains. Is this a fluke of nature, or an
odd apparition that defies expert wisdom?*

A manda was tending her vegetable farm when Marco
and Toby woke up. She usually prepared breakfast for
the boys before she stepped out of the house.

Marco smelled the rice sautéed in oil and garlic and the
fried spicy pork sausages that she usually paired together. The
aroma of the newly brewed, home-grown Arabica coffee wafted
throughout their three-bedroom farmhouse.

"Mama's breakfast dishes are so good, especially her
sausages and omelets," he told his younger brother, who gave
him a thumbs up sign.

"What a great feeling to wake up smelling the delicious
food," Toby said. "She serves our favorite food when we're here
on vacation."

"She cooks Papa's favorite food, too, when he's here during
his off days."

"Is it the boiled meat, potatoes, and vegetables?"

"Yes, it's the boiled beef mixed with potatoes, onions,
garlic, ginger, tomatoes, and other vegetables she calls cocido. I
know you love the hot broth."

"In spite of your love of food, especially Mama's home-cooked meals, you're not gaining weight at all. How do you explain that?"

"My constant activities outdoors and martial arts training honed my body for strength and stamina, not for bulk."

"There seems to be no likeness between us brothers. I mean, you are lean, big-boned, and much taller than I am. And you have the olive skin and Hispanic features of Lolo Gil."

"I'll try to explain it the best way I can, Toby. Mama could give an insight into some of your concerns. We'll ask her when we get the chance. In case you didn't know or have forgotten, Mama's paternal grandfather was the son of a Spanish friar, surnamed Montalvo, who apparently passed his genes to Lolo, to Mama, and to me. In your case, you've likely acquired Papa's genes."

"Our great-grandfather was the son of a Spanish friar? Aren't priests supposed to stay single?"

"Catholic priests are required by the Church to stay unmarried and abstain from sexual relations, but that's not to say that everyone complied with that particular rule. Many of them led double lives during our Spanish colonial history. Some priests continue to violate their creed to this day. Their children were kept away from public scrutiny. I'm not surprised that Mama's maiden name is Mendoza and not Montalvo, as it should have been."

"Some of my friends and classmates have Spanish surnames. Does that mean that their ancestors were Spanish friars?" Toby asked.

"Nearly all colonized Filipinos have Spanish surnames, but that doesn't imply they all have Spanish ancestry. In 1849, Governor General Narciso Claveria passed a decree assigning Spanish surnames to the Filipinos to establish, among other things, better taxpayer identification, as a way to improve the tax collection process. In Papa's hometown in the Bicol Peninsula in the south, many surnames start with the letter F or G. Identical beginning letters of last names were assigned to families in certain localities in accordance with pre-determined combinations. So it was possible to have last names like Gallardo, Gallano, or Gavionza in a town or municipality.

"How come Papa's last name starts with a V and not an F or a G?"

"Town residents probably moved to different places after the Spanish Conquistadores left the country."

While there were no physical similarities between Marco and Toby, they both shared common interests they wanted to pursue as a team; outdoor adventure, and providing assistance to friends and family. Besides managing livestock farming at home, they both possessed unremitting passions that would pull them together for a good part of their lives.

To say that Marco was a serious person, determined to succeed in any venture he chose, would be an understatement. The same could not be said of Toby, who appeared calm and uncomplicated. At age fifteen, and given more time to grow, he could develop into a serious and responsible young man.

Marco's favorite saying was borrowed from the eighteenth century Quaker, Stephan Grellet's Quotations of Kindness. He compressed it into two lines:

"Let me do it now; let me not defer or neglect it, for I shall not pass this way again."

Toby packed some clothes and other personal effects in his knapsack and was on his way to take the public transportation to town to help his friend, Reggie, repair his leaking roof. He wasn't expected to be back until after the job was done. The sun was breaking through the clouds, and he knew he must hurry or else he would miss the early jeepney ride.

In his absence, Marco was responsible for Aladdin's care, and all the work necessary in maintaining their start-up piggery.

Marco cleaned the pig stalls and refilled the water troughs with fresh water. He went to the barn and loaded a few sacks of hog feed into the cart and took them to the stalls. After he filled the feeding troughs with the hog mash, he went to the corral next to their vegetable farm and took care of the needs of Aladdin. That concluded his routine morning chores.

Amanda expected to harvest her farm crops in about two weeks, or when they became market-ready, whichever came first. Marco and Toby, who were home for the school break, would help her with the farm tasks when they were needed. She expected her husband, Olin, to soon get some days off in order to assist them all in getting the farm products ready for market.

Some vegetable varieties are harvested three or four times in a season. Depending on the weather, others can be harvested once or twice a year. Moisture-sensitive vegetables can be harvested just once a year, during the summer months.

When there was an urgent need for help on the vegetable farm, Amanda normally asked Marco or Toby to give her a helping hand. If they were very busy with their responsibilities in taking care of the horse and piggery, she could ask Rosie, her hired farm assistant, for help. This particular morning, Rosie was in the nursery sowing the seeds. Rosie would be all the help she needed for the next three days or so. She would, however, need the boys' help when the seedlings were ready for transplanting to the plots, and especially so during harvest time.

Marco decided that it was time to take to the trail anew. He planned for a short hike to exercise his muscles, and for the sheer pleasure of hiking across the valley and beyond. He planned to be home before the rains returned to soak the countryside.

Expecting to pick blueberries and other wild berries along the way, he packed only light snacks. He filled his canteen with fresh drinking water.

The young man crossed the big valley and walked down a steep canyon trail that led to a narrow plank bridge. The bridge was supported by steel cables, and was anchored to solid rock on both ends of the footbridge.

Silted, brownish water, evident of soil erosion upstream, meandered along the river gorge.

Walking past the bouncy plank bridge, Marco continued to hike the trail leading to a rocky hillside. It seemed like an easy climb but he knew, as he had discovered before, that it was difficult to get past the hill, with the huge boulders that must be sidestepped. It was similar to walking through an inclined maze with the exit at the top.

He reached the berry field, a reasonably level area with green vegetation contrasting with the rocky background. Wild fruit-bearing shrubs such as blueberries, blackberries, raspberries, and other vegetation were randomly scattered over a fairly wide area.

Marco penetrated some of the dense brambles to fill his plastic-lined knapsack, eating some of it until he was full. He sat down briefly to rest and rehydrate. Observing the blueberries that are seasonally abundant, he recalled his mother sharing words that were handed down to her by her father, Gil Mendoza, the retired high school biology teacher and principal of his school.

"The blueberries and other fruit bearing wild shrubs are propagated by birds feeding on the fruits and dispersing the seeds randomly over a wide area."

His grandfather went on to restate the fact that: "The seeds grow on layers of soil formed from particles of weathered rock and decomposed organic material deposited by water and other agents of erosion over a long period of time."

Marco continued to hike until he saw a high, weathered rock wall ahead. Gazing at the cliff, he decided to scale it.

He went higher, and noticed that the rock formation was heavily fractured and craggy, offering a means for novice climbers to reach higher elevation without the need for rock climbing equipment. "So far so good," he said, as he continued his climb.

Midway to the peak of the cliff, he stopped to feast his eyes on the picturesque scenery across the canyon. With the massive Caraballo Mountain Range and its cloud-draped tops providing the backdrop, he marveled as he looked down upon the parallel rows of verdant vegetables of different varieties, neatly strewn across the fertile valley known as "the big valley" or simply "the valley" by the people living in San Antonio and its farming suburbs.

He likened the scenery to artwork on canvas. As he gazed farther down to the west, he saw his bay horse grazing in the meadow. "It's time we ride the trail again, Aladdin."

Patches of dark rain clouds were forming on the horizon. It was a harbinger of impending afternoon tropical rains. A mild northerly wind gusted at thirty-five kilometers per hour.

Not to worry. He planned to hurry home before the expected heavy rains drenched the valley and the surrounding areas. If he were to get caught in the downpour on his way back to the big valley, he would have his raincoat inside his knapsack. He could also seek cover among the trees. A good drenching wouldn't be a problem for him anyhow.

He continued to climb.

Moments later he heard a series of loud, shrieking sounds

from the sky. "What was that?" he whispered. He looked up toward the sky and saw a very large bird, with a white underside and broad wings, fully extended, soaring above the valley. "Those wings are amazing. It must belong to a huge eagle."

It was his first encounter with this magnificent bird of prey. Observing the eye-catching creature in flight, he likened it to a pterodactyl—perhaps because he'd acquired a keen interest in the extinct flying reptile long before.

How strange it is to see this magnificent, winged predator in these mountains. Is this a fluke of nature, or an odd apparition that defies common wisdom? Marco wondered, knowing that the predators' home range was in the faraway Sierra Madre Mountains to the north.

"I hope that mother saw the big bird soar above while working in the farm. If she heard the high-pitched shrieks, she'd look up in the sky without a doubt and behold the rare but matchless sight. I have questions to ask her about the predator when I get home."

Expecting the eagle to circle a little longer in the sky, Marco relieved his tiring left foot by transferring his weight from one leg to the other. The shift also provided him with a more stable foothold. When he regained his sight of the eagle, he was surprised to see the huge bird plunge, like an arrow, and then level off as it came close to the meadow, with wings flapping for balance, and dark talons pushing forward to lunge at a running prey. It snatched the animal on the field with quick, coordinated movements of its wings and claws while retaining momentum to remain on its homeward flight without touching the ground. Marco watched the eagle fly north, in the direction of Mount Malvar, until it was merely a dot on the horizon.

That evening, Amanda served arroz caldo (hot porridge with chicken), sweet potato tops salad, and dried fish for dinner. Marco sipped his evening tea.

Both were quiet, perhaps still mesmerized by the sight of the giant predator they saw in the valley for the first time.

"Mama, did you see a huge eagle hunting prey today?"

"Yes. I would guess it caught a wild rabbit with its claws, although it's impossible to say it was a rabbit for sure, given the speed of the attack and my distance from the predator."

"Hmmm. The eagle must have been very hungry, or it had an eaglet to feed in its nest somewhere," he said. "Is the eagle the largest bird in the world?"

"I've read that monkey-eating eagles are some of the largest and most powerful birds of prey in the world. They are the dominant hunters in the skies and on the ground in our country. Vast areas of hunting ranges are necessary to support their food requirement, particularly when they're feeding their young. They occupy the tier below ours in the food chain, a significant factor that accounts for their huge size."

"What do they eat besides wild rabbits?"

"They hunt reptiles, monkeys, squirrels, hornbills, and other animals endemic to the region. Eagles on other islands of the archipelago hunt flying lemurs, civets, and other animals native to the locality. Generally speaking, their food depends on the faunal assortment, and size of their hunting range," she said. "For example, if the endemics on an eagles' island habitat are composed essentially of brown monkeys, squirrels, and flying lemurs, it follows that brown monkeys, squirrels, and flying lemurs are mainly their leading diet. You follow?"

"Yes of course, Mama."

She further explained to the very attentive Marco that the eagle they saw looked very special. "I'm certain that the predator is our own monkey-eating eagle. No other eagle species of that size is native to the Philippines. Monkey-eating eagles don't live in our forests; they nest and forage in rainforests in the Sierra Madre Mountains to the northeast and on other islands, such as Samar, Leyte, and Mindanao, to the south. I'm really amazed to see the eagle hunt here. All these years, I haven't seen nor heard of a monkey-eating eagle soar, let alone hunt in these mountains—until today."

"Is it true that their numbers are in gradual decline?" he asked.

"It's true, and that's very unfortunate. We read that our rainforests, which are their normal habitat, are disappearing at an alarming rate. We can see that happening in our municipality as well. Trees are indiscriminately cut for lumber, land is cleared of trees to provide spaces for houses and buildings, and forests are burned for agricultural needs. If this trend continues, the monkey-eating eagle and other birds and animals whose existence depend on our forest resources will someday disappear from our islands. Your father told me that when Northern Consolidated Copper Mines constructed a new road to access a satellite project of theirs, all the trees near the road disappeared in a matter of weeks."

"Are you telling me that the mining company aided in the destruction of our forests when they constructed the new road?"

"No, that's not what I said. Roads must be built if necessary, but existing laws enacted for the protection of our forests should be enforced to the full extent. Enforcement of the law remains to be the problem," she said "There's also the need to educate the people on forest conservation."

"Are there law's that protect the eagles, too?"

"I'm sure there are existing laws for their protection that we are not aware of. Then again, having laws without strict enforcement is tantamount to having none at all.

"In 1969, through the efforts of noted Filipino scientist Dr. Dioscoro Rabor, and the world renowned aviator and conservationist Charles Lindberg, who represented the World Wildlife Fund, the monkey-eating eagle conservation program was launched by the Philippine Eagle Foundation. The non-profit foundation was formed to help save the endangered species. Dr. Rabor made it known to the world that the population of the monkey-eating eagle was in a dangerous decline. Mr. Lindbergh was so captivated by the monkey-eating eagle that he rightly gave it the title, The World's Noblest Flier."

"I've learned many things from our question and answer session. Actually, it was my questions and your answers. Thanks a lot, Mama. We should have more of these exchanges."

Marco went straight to his room to visualize the huge and majestic bird and to think of ways he could help in the monkey-eating eagle conservation program, especially when he became a full-fledged biologist.

It was late when he slept that night. The form of the giant eagle was fresh in his mind, and he could picture the eagle with its long wingspan circling the sky, shrieking, diving, and grabbing its prey. The big bird truly fascinated him.

Amanda's disclosure to Marco of the news about the eagles' conservation program lit his eyes with excitement. She had observed that Marco became fascinated with the eagle right after watching it hunt in the valley. "Once he's focused on something that catches his attention, he's so persistent and unrelenting in pursuing it, no matter what it takes or where it will lead him," she acknowledged. "He's an aspiring biologist, and I suppose monkey-eating eagles, like all other animals, are of interest to him."

Marco couldn't wait to watch the magnificent bird soar above the valley again. He would love to hear its high-pitched whistles, too.

"Do you know if there are books about the monkey-eating eagle for sale and if so, where can I buy one?" he asked Amanda.

"There must be bigger bookstores in Manila that carry such books in their inventory. I'll write Alan, a business associate and former high school classmate of mine, to look around and buy you a book or two. Depending on their in-stock availability, he could send the books along with the farm products I ordered from Agro Products Marketing Company, his start-up company.

"Most books don't delve on a particular eagle species. They describe and present pictorials of a few eagles in the world and how they compare with others. Some books may even include other birds of prey, such as hawks and owls, lumped in with the eagles in a single chapter. Or they may be grouped according to their scientific classifications to include non-predatory birds. A few pages of the book may include more detailed pictures of and narratives on some species: the bald eagle, the harpy eagle, the golden eagle, or the monkey-eating eagle, to name a few. This last one might interest you the most. Whichever eagle books are in stock, I'm certain you'll enjoy reading them."

Years ago in her high school biology class, Amanda was assigned to make a report on the monkey-eating eagle species. The central point of her narrative would be the eagles' habitat, their prey, and other important matters affecting their continued existence.

She researched her subject in the school library and even traveled to a nearby town to interview Mr. Jesus Madera, a retired wildlife photographer who once photographed monkey-eating eagles and other birds of prey for publication. Considered mysterious at times by his peers, the wildlife photographer was known for his extensive knowledge of predatory birds. He gave Amanda a transverse flute, fashioned from bamboo.

He claimed the special-made woodwind instrument could generate high-pitched whistle sounds similar to the predators' shrieks that would attract their attention, and even entice them to obey certain hand signals or voice commands. "I used the wind gadget to tame and even charm the eagles before I took their pictures for my magazine," he said.

"I probably won't need it for that same reason, but I'll keep it as a gift. Thank you very much for your help. Maraming salamat po." In appreciation of his assistance, she gave him two boxes of Alhambra cigars and a big bottle of Tanduay rum.

In Amanda's report, the effect of deforestation on the continued existence of the monkey-eating eagles loomed large. She concluded her report by stressing the fact that if excessive logging and burning of forests for agriculture remained unmanaged, the eagles would likely disappear someday from the islands' habitats in the archipelago.

Her narrative of the monkey-eating eagles was good enough to merit a one-hundred-percentile grade. Unfortunately, she had lost her only copy of that school report, and the book and magazines she used as references. Had she taken the time to file her important school materials, Marco would have the resources to gain knowledge of the eagles, and he might not need to order the books.

It's quite interesting to note that if Amanda were to write a new report on the current issues impinging on the monkey-eating eagles' survival, it would be similar to what she wrote in high school almost two decades ago.

Marco stayed close to home to help his mother and Rosie on the vegetable farm after taking care of the piggery and the horse.

Aware that his mother had work backlog and that she needed to catch up, he didn't go trail hiking. He provided her with an extra hand in the nursery, but more importantly, he wanted to show her his appreciation for ordering the books he wanted to read.

Amanda was confident that Rosie's help on the farm would suffice, and together they could catch up with the work pileup. She would, however, welcome help of any kind from Marco or Toby when they had time to spare.

The two books that Amanda requested that Alan buy for Marco arrived in the mail two weeks later, along with a letter to express his thanks to Amanda for the farm products she ordered. He promised that the fertilizer and hog feed would be delivered in a week at the latest. In the P.S. section of the letter, he mentioned that the books were the better ones he could find in any of the bookstores he visited.

Marco managed to find time to read them during the day, but he did most of his reading before he went to bed at night.

CHAPTER 6

ON THE TRAIL OF THE EAGLE

These men must be from Mars. They are nuts. I never heard of treasures buried in these mountains. If there were, it would be like searching for a needle in a haystack. I better get going.

W hen he finished his morning piggery chores, Marco went to the barn to take stock of his horse-riding paraphernalia. He took the old McClellan saddle off the improvised rack, dropped it on his lap, and cleaned it. Dusting it was a good excuse to inspect it. He placed it back on the rack, expecting an imminent need for it. He next checked the condition of the bridle, stirrups, hackamore, and all leather pieces and sundry hanging from the pegs on the wall. "They've always been in good condition and are ready to be used anytime we need them, but it pays to check them in case an item or two are missing or may need repair."

He visited Aladdin grazing near their vegetable farm. Once he opened the corral gate, the seven-year-old gelding created a mild commotion, neighing and trotting toward Marco. The horse looked ready to take to the mountain trails with him. Or was it that he smelled the brown sugar in Marco's palm? Both statements could be true.

"We haven't been on an extended trail ride in the mountains," he said to the horse, offering him a handful of unrefined brown sugar. "But we'll take the trail again in the next day or two, after I've finished reading my newly purchased eagle books." He reached up to hug the horse by the neck.

When Marco and Toby took Aladdin on a short trail ride, Gizmo, their German shepherd dog, tagged along as a regular member of the trekking team.

He had finished reading both books in record time and passed them on to his mother, who pored over the pages without saying a word. She smiled and dropped the books on top of her bedroom shelf, her way of telling Marco that she would read the books when she crossed out most of the "must-do things" on her list.

At daybreak, Marco cinched up his horse with attention to detail in anticipation of a rough terrain ride. He tied his camping gear, food, and miscellaneous supplies—including Gizmo's food—to the front and back of the saddle and left the valley on horseback.

The day before, he told his mother that he expected to be back in four days, but his absence could take a day longer, depending on the weather. "Gizmo and I will run out of food if we're not back in seven days, Mama. Please take care of the piggery while I'm away."

Marco patted his horse and whispered, "I need your strength and patience to help me track down the giant eagle I saw hunting for food here in the valley not very long ago."

He made half a dozen detours to steer clear of narrow foot bridges or steep slopes and deep ravines that horses cannot cross safely. He stayed away from swamps and wet paddies that could mimic quicksand.

Years ago, he witnessed a horse get stuck in a wet rice paddy. He tried to help the owner pull the horse out of the mud one leg at a time but when the horse struggled to free himself, he went deeper into the mud. He stayed with the colt to calm him down while the owner went for help. With ropes, pulleys and lumber, it took half the village to free the pony from the muddy trap.

Many times, he dismounted and led the horse uphill or downhill across gullies and creeks, expertly handling the leather, and giving voice commands to relax and control the spirited steed. Knowing the area and the detours well, Marco took the longer route to make it safer and more convenient for him and his horse.

He followed certain pathways when he took the trail in the mountains, and seldom deviated from his tried-and-true route unless he was convinced that the alternative was more practical in terms of safety and saving time.

His inquisitive mind and daring lifestyle caused him to be prone to accidents. Save for a few bruises here and there, he usually emerged unscathed.

While it had been a challenge to ride or lead his horse on this rugged terrain, he knew that once they reached the ridge above the old logging road, it would be much easier for him and the team. They could move across the mountains on the beaten trail without dismounting the rest of the way.

He rode his mount without a major hitch.

Like a scout, Gizmo was always on the move, behind or ahead of Marco and Aladdin.

It had been a while since his last trek to the heart of the wilderness without Toby and their friends. He stopped Aladdin to listen to the whispering leaves as they swayed with the cooling breeze. "The loneliness and pleasures of solitude," he reflected.

It was late in the afternoon when he saw a vegetated area near a flowing spring water. He set up camp there to give Aladdin and Gizmo a much-needed rest. Notwithstanding his well-toned physique, mounting and dismounting his horse many times that morning had taken its toll on him.

Marco allowed the full length of the short rope for Aladdin to have access to water and graze on the green pasture. He fed

Gizmo and ate his warmed, cooked food. They rested by the fire and soon fell asleep in his tent. Gizmo slept inside the tent and near the exit, always ready to attack if an unwanted intruder showed up.

It rained late that night. He woke up to find Aladdin protected in some measure against the wind and rain by a clump of trees.

Well rested and anxious to start another day in the forest, Marco had roasted sweet potatoes and dried salted fish for breakfast. He provided for the needs of his horse and dog.

Tall and bearded treasure hunter Dick Striecher and his pint-sized partner, Hiro Shimada, were studying a general map of Northern Luzon, showing the route of General Tomoyoki Yamashita when he hastily retreated from the Allied Forces during World War II. During his speedy tactical withdrawal to the mountain stronghold, Yamashita and his army were said to have buried the treasures in gold, silver, and precious stones that were previously taken from Japanese occupied east and southeast Asian countries. The Yamashita treasures, intended to be shipped to Japan to help their war effort, were hurriedly buried in the mountains for fear that they would fall into the hands of the advancing Allied Army that was hot on his trail.

When Hiro went to Japan to visit his relatives the past year, he obtained the map from his great uncle, Yoshiaki Shimada. This map, one of the estimated hundreds acquired by treasure hunters from supposed war historians and eyewitnesses, and from Japanese sources, was alleged to have been obtained by Yoshiaki's father from T/Sgt. Shige Namoki, who fought with the 14th Imperial Japanese Army in the Philippines under the command of Yamashita.

The treasure hunt was funded by Mr. Roger Gardner, a wealthy American businessman who had thus far been resolute in his belief that one day he and his team would find some of the fortune that had been stashed away by the invading forces. They had uncovered Japanese military swords, guns, bayonets, helmets, ammunitions, and other rusty relics while they were digging tunnels in search of treasures in the Cordillera Mountains. The treasure hunters would contend that the swords might have commanded an excellent trade opportunity in Japan if they had serial numbers, such as those issued to officers of the Japanese military. Only unmarked, Japanese standard issues were found, and so were kept as souvenirs.

Hiro, with his newly acquired treasure map in his hands, convinced Roger and Dick to transfer their treasure-hunting operations from the Cordilleras to the South Caraballo Mountains. Hiro had learned that bloody battles between the American forces and Yamashita's army had taken place in those mountains. The map showed the route of the Japanese general as he marched through that area during his retreat.

Because of the confusion created by inaccuracies exhibited on the map, Dick and Hiro hired a couple of villagers who knew the mountains in order to verify some of the landmarks featured on the map. Many others were hired as diggers to excavate and retrieve the purported loot.

Hiro repeated what he had told Dick at one time. "The treasures were packed in separate caches and stored in different tunnels that the Japanese soldiers, with the help of Filipino civilians, excavated in a hurry. After the caches were hoarded underground, the hired workers used ropes and pulleys to roll huge rocks to seal the openings. Some of them were trip-mined by the Japanese military. When the job was done, the hired workers were directed to walk to a secluded area where they were shot to death, safeguarding the secret of the buried treasures." And so goes the saga.

"I hear you," Dick said. "I do believe that Yamashita's treasures are buried somewhere in these mountains. Our job is to find them."

Dick used a metal detector to find out what was hidden behind the big rock. He was thrilled to inform Hiro of the anomaly that registered on the gauge as he passed behind the rock. "As soon as I repeated the process, the detector hummed the same sweet note," he said.

They were ready to excavate behind the rock, and they realized that if this was the big find, they were prepared to get their hands on the gold, silver, and other precious stones.

Marco saw the men milling around a big rock as he passed through. He dismounted from his horse and maintained a safe distance from the strangers while checking on their activities. He was convinced that they were friendly because of their deportment, and the fact that not one of them was holding a rifle in his hands—just picks, crowbars, and shovels. "If they turn out to be feisty or wish to be left alone, then I'm on my way out. If not, I'll greet them and leave. Who knows, we may have a common interest we can talk about."

"Who goes there?" Dick said.

"My name's Marco Vega and I'm from San Antonio. I'm on my way north to Mount Malvar. This is my horse, Aladdin, and over there is Gizmo, my dog."

"What's on Mount Malvar that you might want to share with us?" Hiro asked.

"I'm a biology major and I'm tracking down a giant eagle. I thought I might be able to encounter the winged predator there because I watched it soar in that direction a couple of times. What's behind that rock you seem to be scrutinizing?"

"We're treasure hunters. I'm Dick and he's Hiro. These are our men. We're starting to dig behind this rock because we believe there are gold, silver, and precious stones buried here."

"Remember me when you hit it big!" Marco said. "Good luck."

"Track the eagle and have fun along the way," Hiro replied.

"These men must be from Mars. They are nuts. I never heard of treasures buried in these mountains. If there were, it would be searching for a needle in a haystack. I better get going."

He rode past the old logging road, took the short ascent to the ridge, and trotted on the trail through patches of hedges and trees.

Marco's quiet ride was broken by a series of high-pitched whistles from the sky. The giant eagle was soaring above, set to seek out its next prey.

Well inside the predator's immense foraging area, Marco's current location was one of the areas he expected the eagle to hunt. He was not surprised to encounter the eagle there, although he was intrigued to find that his team had arrived at the ridge so close to the winged predator's domain; the sole reason he rode out to the mountains with Aladdin and Gizmo.

He watched in awe as the eagle hunted in the valley. His consequent actions bore the subtle signs of enthrallment with the giant predator.

The young man quickly dismounted, pulled Aladdin aside and secured him to a tree. He ran to the clearing to get a better view of the predator diving to attack a prey on the ground. The huge eagle pulled up from its dive with its powerful claws positioned to snatch up an unsuspecting monitor lizard.

Through all the commotion, Marco saw Gizmo run to attack the winged predator as it approached the ground to grab its prey. The canine couldn't come close to the eagle as it swiftly continued its flight home, gripping its prey without touching the ground.

"The eagle could have killed Gizmo. I'm glad the predator had the prey long in its sights before Gizmo attacked."

Marco watched the flight of the eagle to determine as best he could where it would end up. "Will it land or continue its flight?" he wondered.

He ran to the clearing on his right to stay clear of the bunch of trees obstructing his sight. The lad had a clear view of the predator as it flew north toward the mountains.

Marco stood there, unmoving, his eyes transfixed on the eagle in flight even as it became a fleck in the sky. Minutes passed. Marco, still gazing at the eagle, would attest that he saw the fleck disappear as it came close to Mount Malvar. "The eagle must have landed near the tall, rocky structure or thereabouts."

He continued to ride north, hoping to have another close look at the eagle near the spot where it had vanished.

Marco watched a flock of blackbirds fly around and across them. He felt a sense of foreboding in that moment, perhaps a warning that something untoward awaited him if he continued his journey.

He believed in dreams and their meanings but not in omens, good or bad. He never gave black birds or black cats a second thought simply because he did not harbor portentous feelings.

"Let's get going," he gently prodded Aladdin and Gizmo.

The weather had looked threatening since early that morning. The tranquility in the forest was broken by stiff winds blowing against the leaves of trees and hedges. The sky was getting dark and menacing, coupled with ominous rumblings echoing across the distant ridges and canyons—all signs of an impending rainstorm.

A typhoon appeared headed their way and it gave Marco a bit of concern. It could set back the time of his planned encounter with the giant eagle in its home territory by at least a few days. Anticipating miserably wet and windy days ahead, he would need to find shelter until the storm passed.

Marco knew from experience that the storm would reach land before nightfall, or as late as the following morning.

In one of his outdoor trips with Toby and their friends, he recalled that there was an old, abandoned gold mill, along with remnants of building structures that stood on a mountainside not far from the northbound trail. They had passed through the site on their way to Campground One at one time.

"The roofed area could certainly provide us protection from the rainstorm. It's worth the trouble going the extra kilometers. We'll weather the storm there." He deviated from his current route to get to the gold mill. They would need to hurry, lest they be buffeted by the strong winds on their way.

Taking a detour from the trail, Marco blazed a new pathway to a creek. While leading his horse upstream on a sandy bank, he spotted a huge monitor lizard atop a big rock. He was alarmed by the loud rustle as the reptile dove and quickly disappeared into the thick vegetation at the foot of the boulder. When he reached the big rock, he noticed a cavity etched through it. He peeked inside the man-made cave and found old coffins carved from logs stored therein. They were stocked two-high and two-across in order to conserve space. He guessed that the coffins were more than a century old. "It's amazing how the people back then, without explosives at their disposal, were able to painstakingly cut through the solid rock with only primitive tools to work with," he figured. "The coffins are still very much intact except for some deformation, which would be expected after all the years that have passed. I can't wait to tell Toby that I've seen a revered relic in this ancient land of the dead. I suppose he would want to visit this place someday." Upon closer inspection of the burial chamber, he thought it was clever of the stone whittlers to make use of a vertical crack across the rock as the break plane to chisel through. "It certainly helped them bore through the hard andesite boulder."

The team ascended the hill to reach the ridge-straddling municipal road that connects to the private mine road and the gold mill. In light of the infrequent maintenance work allotted to the mine road, it could only be used by hikers or travelers on horseback during this peak time of seasonal and monsoon rains.

They arrived at the rusty gold mill long before dark. Marco noticed that only a small fraction of the mill structure was still standing after years of abandonment. The cracking concrete floor was intact and surprisingly, a third of its area was still under a roof.

He collected dry wood branches and started a fire to keep their makeshift camp warm and more livable.

While he was out on the slopes gathering more firewood prior to the impending downpour, he observed that there was a healthy growth of vegetation around the vicinity of the gold mill. It had not been that way since their last hike-by in the area. "I'll cut some grass for Aladdin to munch on while we're inside our roofed camp and if he needs more food, he can graze outside where I can watch him.

Gazing at the dry creek bed, he noticed damaged sluice boxes lying near the bottom of the rust-stained bedrock.

"Growing up in the mine, I've learned from friends that flowing water is necessary to separate tiny gold particles from a stockpile of low-grade, gold-laden sand or ground gold ore while spread out on a series of inclined burlap-lined sluice boxes. They called it sluicing," he recalled.

"Hmm! That figures," he said, as he remembered some nuggets of wisdom from friends in the mine who were experienced in the gold-scavenging process. He saw remnants of a crude bamboo water pipeline fastened to tree trunks or anchored to hillside rocks. People who live not too far from here attempted to recover minute gold particles left from the previous gold mining operations. Water needed for the gold recovery process was piped from sources upstream.

Marco was puzzled that with the frequent rain and typhoon pounding the area, the creek bed was bone-dry. "Water that flowed along the creek must have been diverted to another drainage system."

He took Aladdin and Gizmo upstream to drink and to fill his water canteen.

As he sat down to rest and wait for the gathering storm to consummate its fury, he watched Aladdin graze quietly between snorts. Marco recalled the events that led to the acquisition of the horse two years ago when he was fifteen years old. It was that time his family moved from the mine to their farm home in the valley. He'd had fun moments on many occasions when he and his cousin, Jonah Valverde, roped horses and rode them for amusement.

One particular bay stallion was often ridden by the boys and later became their favorite. He stood out as the best among the horses they rode. The man who owned the bay likely knew that the boys were riding it without his knowledge, let alone his consent, but for some reason he did not make an attempt to stop them from having their fun. For this, Marco and Jonah were forever indebted to the man.

Many mornings, when the dewdrops on the meadow started to glisten against the sun as it rose above the eastern horizon, the boys knew it was time to have fun with their favorite horse. They would walk slowly toward the grazing stallion while Jonah pulled one end of the rope slung over Marco's shoulder. Spread seven meters apart, they would drag the rope on each end and approached the stallion on both flanks. Once the slackened rope was directly under the horse's head, the boys raised it on both ends.

With the taut rope touching his neck, the horse was kept at bay until one of them swung the rope from one end to complete the loop around his neck. From that same rope, they knotted a makeshift bridle to control the bay stallion before riding it. They took turns riding the horse bareback on a fast gallop across the meadow before releasing him back to the grazing grounds.

"It's payback time in your favor, my dear stallion." Marco patted the horse while he showed his appreciation by giving him brown sugar.

Now and then, the boys amused themselves by roping other horses and riding them bareback. One cold and foggy morning, they corralled a young and spirited stallion. They found him reactive at the slightest provocation. As soon as Marco was atop the horse's back, he bucked like a bronco and galloped through the trees and thick bushes, leaving him on the ground with cuts and bruises over parts of his body. The boys realized that they had found more than their match in the young stallion.

When his grandfather learned from Amanda about Marco's profound fondness of horses and the odd things he and Jonah did to be able to ride them, he bought a gelding for him and Toby. Jonah was told that he could take Aladdin for a trail ride whenever he could find time for it.

The rain was now heavy and sustained. The wind whistled and howled through the trees and shrubs all night. During the typhoon's furious onslaught, Marco awoke in the middle of the night and at the crack of dawn to check on Aladdin, who was tethered under the roofed section next to his tent.

The mill structure seemed to be holding out from the winds, despite its creaky condition. He determined that the mill was constructed on the side of a mountain that was protected by natural windbreakers. "No big wonder this nearly desolate remnant of progress in the past endured through the years."

Still cooped in solitude for the third day, the team held out in their camp inside the old mill as campfire smoke billowed into the sky through an opening in the roof.

Then, even as the sky was dark and dismal, Marco heard distant thunder rolls that opened his eyes with delight. "Sounds like the big storm's ebbing tonight," he whispered to Gizmo, who was in the midst of deep slumber inside the tent.

Counting the days and hours the group spent in their camp, Marco estimated that it had taken some fifty-five hours for the big storm to pass. The rain and the whistling winds subsided that morning.

Once more, the sun peeked through the lingering clouds and shone upon the gleaming countryside to usher the start of a new and promising day.

From their rainstorm sanctuary, Marco took a quick look at the old mine site around the corner before leaving the area and heading back to the northbound trail on the way to Mount Malvar.

The haulage tunnel, the main entry to the abandoned underground gold mine, was permanently sealed with a concrete bulkhead, but allowed water to drain through a drain pipe embedded at the bottom of the concrete. Trees abounded above the portal site, with a few jutting out around the gravel-filled area between the half-decayed rail ties. There were bits and pieces of a rail-track system upon which three-ton car trains loaded with gold ore rolled to the mill for extraction of the precious metals; gold, and silver.

Forlorn and deserted, nothing remained on the site except the three rusty one-ton cars that adorned the portal area and the protuberant reinforced concrete foundations of non-existent buildings. These were reminiscent of a bygone era of corporate gold mining in the region.

Holding Aladdin's reins, Marco stood somberly, recreating in his mind the phantom images of workers moving about their activities when the mining operation was at its peak. He had visions of himself mingling amongst his thought-up apparitions, but that wouldn't be so, as his abstractions were based on experiences growing up in another mine, in another time.

He once fancied himself working in an underground mine like his father had, but that boyhood dream had lost its luster and while it faded away, his vision of becoming a biologist blossomed.

Back on the trail, he was pleased to be mobile again after the brief respite, as were Aladdin and Gizmo, who appeared eager to leave the area.

Farther north, he discovered a shuttered drainage tunnel—part of the Lagrimas Mining Complex—that could have doubled as a ventilation duct in the previous scheme of operations. Permanently barricaded with old rails and concrete, the portal was discharging significant amounts of water into a ravine. It was coursed through a concrete drainage channel on the hillside.

In spite of his growing up in a similar mine, the inquisitive young man could not understand where the large volume of water was trickling from.

Drawn by the striking scenery below and intent on delving further into the water source issue, he decided to take a closer look of the area. He dismounted and led Aladdin to graze off-trail. While his horse was efficient on the trail, he couldn't take him to the steep slopes. He strapped his knapsack and walked downhill with Gizmo.

CHAPTER 7
A STARTLING DISCOVERY

Through his lenses clearly, he witnessed a jaw-dropping scenery that grabbed his full attention—tall cannabis "hemp" plants were neatly sticking out on the rolling hectares of land.

Descending the rugged landscape past the gushing water, Marco was quite surprised when he saw a wisp of smoke coming from a level clearing below, just above the river. He had not seen nor spoken to anyone since his meeting with Dick, Hiro, and the rest of the treasure hunters several days earlier. Where there's smoke, there's fire, and where there's fire, there must be campers in the area, he thought. Or perhaps more treasure hunters searching for gold, silver, and precious gemstones. Adjusting the antique pair of larga vista (binoculars) he inherited from his Lolo Gil, he found that the smoke was venting out from a hut below.

"Campers like us love the outdoors, but why would they put up a semi-permanent, thatched shack when they could have used portable tents as temporary camps? Without doubt, they don't intend to stay there for an extended period of time, unless they are also looking for buried treasures in the area."

He saw a water pipeline hugging the hillside. Segments of the pipeline were fastened to tree trunks or anchored on the slopes where there were no trees. He descended farther to investigate what it was intended for.

The scene below further revealed that the water coming out of the tunnel was coursed through a concrete ditch and impounded in a makeshift holding reservoir, which was made out of metal barrels and piped to an unseen location beyond the ridge.

Marco had to unravel one last part of the puzzle. He needed to find the beneficiary of the piped water in order to solve the mystery.

Through his lenses clearly, he witnessed a jaw-dropping scenery that grabbed his full attention—tall cannabis "hemp" plants were neatly sticking out on the rolling hectares of land.

He noted that the extent of the marijuana farm could not be fully determined from his current location. The vast majority of the plants were grown on the other side of the ridge hidden from the trail; he could tell that the crop was immense.

The hemp farm could easily be sighted by a keen outdoorsman equipped with a pair of larga vista, especially one like him who would wander off the trail to view the stunning countryside below and observe the water streaming out of the tunnel.

Irrigating the illegal plants during the dry months would be mandatory.

He and his camping friends had come across a few marijuana plantations during some of their outdoor treks, but they were not quite as large as this patch.

To remain unseen by the pot growers, Marco laid face down on a berm overlooking the camp and the plantation. Alternating his focus on both areas of interest, he thought the operation below was intriguing enough to justify the extra time he would have to spend there.

Armed men, who could have passed as small game or treasure hunters in the eyes of unsuspecting mountain hikers, showed detachment from all activities that could have been linked to the care and proliferation of the illegal plants. The tall shrubs were conveniently grown away from their hut. Unless apprehending authorities could show hard evidence to prove their complicity in breaking the law, the pot growers would be off the hook.

Marco observed a pair of guards going in and out of the shack. He estimated five men to be there, including two night guards sleeping inside.

Totally engrossed in watching the activities below, or at times wondering about the lack thereof, Marco became oblivious to his surroundings. He didn't notice a roving patrolman approaching his position. He was startled when Gizmo began to growl. He picked up the warning that a prowler was in their midst. When he turned on his back to face and identify the threat, he was terrified to see a gunman with an assault rifle pointed at him. The youngster rolled down the hillside, narrowly escaping bullets that whizzed past him. He caught a glimpse of Gizmo taking off from the ground to attack the guard and knocking him down. The dog locked his jaws on the man's trigger hand while the shooter struggled to get back on his feet. In the ensuing action, the rifle came loose and landed in the bushes below.

Marco scrambled back to help Gizmo. He knocked the guard to the ground with a side-thrust kick, but that didn't seem to slow him down. The sentry got up quickly, with his arms flailing, but Marco managed to either block or evade his blows. He gave the sentry what he deserved—left and right karate punches that found their marks and finally knocked him out.

Marco slung the rifle on his back after he made sure that the safety mechanism was locked. He zigzagged down the hill to avoid becoming an easy target in case another guard appeared and started firing at him.

Gizmo left the guard on the berm while the latter was regaining consciousness. He caught up with Marco on the slopes.

Responsive but woozy, the sentry went to their camp below to report the incident to their leader. While another guard treated his hand injuries to stop the bleeding and prevent infection, the leader and two other men grabbed their rifles and began to chase Marco. The injured guard was in no condition to continue his assigned job and stayed in camp.

Marco continued to run toward the river, with Gizmo alongside. He was aware that it would not be easy to escape from the drug traffickers now that they had found that their criminal operation was breached. He expected the gunmen to be on his tail until he was caught or killed.

The pair were treading water downstream when they heard shots fired by the drug dealers. They had to keep running to maintain a safe distance from their pursuers to stay alive.

He crossed the river and ascended the hill, looking for a place to hide from the armed men. After navigating through half a kilometer of rugged spillways and gulches, he realized that he should have stayed on the river and continued to wade on the knee-deep water. Having misjudged the terrain, he found that eluding the drug traffickers was never easy on the slopes. Besides that, there was no place to take cover on the open landscape with sparse vegetation. He and his dog could easily be fired upon on that hillside. He could return fire using the seized AR-15 rifle if he had to; an option that would need a quick resolution, if his or Gizmo's life were in imminent danger.

Sergeant Rios, a friend of Marco's who was once assigned as a constabulary officer at the Northern Consolidated Copper Mine, taught him how to use a similar AR-15 rifle when the boy and his family lived in the mining compound. Unclipping the ammo magazine, the constable allowed him to take it home to practice on the assembly and disassembly of its parts. Amanda ordered Marco to return the weapon after learning from Toby that Marco had a rifle in his possession.

He learned how to use the M1 Garand rifle when he was a color guard in his ROTC class at the City of Pines University. That weapon was from the past and was completely different from the one that was slung over his shoulder.

Back on the river, Marco and Gizmo fared much better and managed to increase their distance from their pursuers.

Marco heard more rifle fires, and was still unsure how far their lead was. However, they still might have been within rifle range of the trigger-happy men. Assessing the sounds made by the ricocheting slugs, he felt that they seemed to have a comfortable separation from their pursuers.

The faint roar of a waterfall was audible miles downstream. The din grew louder, rapidly developing into a thunderous roar as Marco and Gizmo progressed down the watercourse. The raging water rushed over the rocky stream, forming white and foamy spray while working its way to the brink and crashing down to the churning pool nearly sixty meters below the channel.

Mindful that the gunmen were no slouches when it came to mobility across the rough terrain, Marco suspected that they might be closing in on them. Moreover, the locale was their zone of operation, and they seemed quite familiar with all the nooks and crannies of the area.

He realized that he did not have the luxury of time to stand back and plan his next move. He pulled Gizmo's canvas collar while he stepped closer to the side of the falls. He looked up and quickly whispered a prayer or two.

Using the huge boulder on one side of the falls as a platform, he held Gizmo's collar tightly and jumped into the bubbly pool below. It took him a couple of seconds to reach the water, and twice as much time to get back to the surface. It could have been the longest six or seven seconds of his life, ever. Still grasping Gizmo's collar, they swam through the turbulence, walked to the riverbank, and hid behind the big rocks. They then took a much needed rest.

He resumed running along the river bank, praying that the thicker growth of vegetation above would provide him a spot to hide from his pursuers. He clambered up the hills again. There, he came across a stockpile of broken rocks that were not completely washed away by the river run-offs during the big rainstorms. His years in the mine taught him that the shape, size, and color of the rocks in the pile indicated that they had originated from a deep underground excavation that was driven with the use of explosives. That could mean one thing—a deep tunnel existed not far from where he stood. Upon closer inspection of the area, he found partly exposed timbers of an old tunnel, covered with vines. He pulled some of the vegetation to clear out the portal. Judging from the size of the opening, he guessed that it could be an old exploration tunnel from long ago, similar to what he had seen before in another place. The opening was barricaded with timbers that were rotting. He kicked at a piece of it, and enough space opened up for him and his dog to get through.

"Between bullets and an abandoned tunnel, I'll chose an abandoned tunnel anytime," he whispered while he stroked his dog's neck. "You saved my life when you attacked the gunman. Thank you, Gizmo; I owe you one."

He held his dog by his collar again, and this time pushed him through the partly blocked portal and into the tunnel. Burdened by his knapsack and the rifle slung across his back, he wedged his slim body through the tight opening to get in. "I'm so relieved that we're no longer in rifle range of those murderous men and I won't have to fire back at them."

The three armed pursuers plodded downstream past the

portal area. They dodged the waterfalls by skirting around the hillside above the river, spending more time traversing the hills and spillways, thus allowing Marco and Gizmo to gain more ground. It became obvious that the leader of the marijuana traffickers preferred not to jump down the falls into the turbulent river, confident that they would eventually gain ground on their quarry. He ordered a guard to go back and check the tunnel opening for signs of a breach, or any evidence that revealed the man and his dog were inside.

The guard saw fresh footprints and what looked like a dog's paw marks. He found bushes freshly pulled out, and a section of the timber barricade broken. He aimed his assault rifle through the broken timber and let loose several bursts of fire. The slugs merely hit the bend of the tunnel and ricocheted harmlessly.

The men on the river joined the other at the portal area when they heard the gunshots. They were certain that the fresh footprints and broken timber were positive indications that the intruder and his dog went inside the tunnel. They fired a few short bursts at strategic points underground. "Ilibing sila," said the boss, ordering his men to bury them.

Reinforcing the old timber barricade, the thugs effectively closed the entrance to the tunnel. They then stacked a layer of rocks outside the barricade to ensure that the interloper and his dog were permanently entombed.

Inside the tunnel, Marco felt the flow of underground air coming from the portal. Based on that finding, his good sense suggested that there had to be an opening at the other end of the tunnel. That would explain why there was a continuity of air flow. He had been warned by his dad not to enter abandoned underground openings unless the tunnel was naturally vented, otherwise, toxic gases would proliferate inside and would cause gas poisoning.

Everything looked good from that point on. They would be safe from the guns of the ill-intentioned pot growers, and there was enough food inside his knapsack to last them a few days. More importantly, there was air to breathe inside the tunnel. The next task was to find the other opening and break out to the outside world.

He sat and took out his flashlight and a box of matches wrapped in plastic to keep them dry. Illuminating the dark underground chamber, he soon saw for the first time what seemed to be an endless passageway through the rock. "This is worse than imprisonment in a dungeon if there's no means of escape at the other end," he roared in dismay. "At least I'm not chained against the wall."

He noticed that they were in the secondary tunnel that branched out from the main opening. Testing the air flow alternately in both openings, faint smoke from his lighted match revealed that only the secondary tunnel showed an air draft. "The main conduit must have caved in somewhere and sealed the opening, or for some reason, tunneling work must have been discontinued. That means I must focus my search for the other opening on this secondary passageway. The air flow will lead us to freedom."

Marco was hungry. He opened a can of corned beef and took out some dried food and water from his knapsack. He shared them with Gizmo.

It had been hectic all day. He was tired after being chased by the drug dealers and felt the need to rest. He would continue the search for an open escape route later. He turned off his flashlight to conserve batteries.

The team resumed walking farther in. They plowed across three partial cave-ins and waded through several pools of water. It is indeed a longer tunnel than I had anticipated, he thought. He couldn't tell what time it was, but a good approximation would be around late afternoon to early evening. They continued to walk for two more hours or so, cleaning debris away with his bare hands in order to squeeze in through the caved sections. When his body clock intuited that it was past bedtime, Marco decided that it was time to catch some sleep. He rested his hand on Gizmo's shoulder to keep him from going astray as he often did.

When he woke up, he was terrified that Gizmo was missing. He turned his flashlight on and started looking for his dog. "Where did he go? Gizmo!" he yelled repeatedly. Moments later, he saw his dog running toward him with his tail wagging. "Don't you ever scare me like that again," he said. "You must be in search of water to drink." He offered the dog water from his knapsack.

Marco discovered that Gizmo had been busy chasing away a pack of rats that kept coming back while he was asleep. Sniffing the empty can of corned beef that he tossed on the tunnel floor, the rats went wild that night.

He opened a can of beans and shared it with his dog. He craved more food, but he had to conserve in case they would need to spend more time underground than expected. More dry food was stashed away in a supply bag tied to his saddle, but that would not be retrieved until they were out of the tunnel.

As soon as they walked away, the rats came back for the empty cans of food that were left behind. One can had some leftover food Marco decided to share with them.

Working his way into the depths of the tunnel, Marco encountered yet another obstacle. Timber supports knocked by caved rocks blocked the opening. Marco commenced to remove the materials underneath, one piece at a time, to free up enough space at the top for him to squeeze through. "If I can get across, so can Gizmo—with ease." Without tools or equipment to dispose of the rocks and timber, it took him more than two hours to finish the job.

He replenished his canteen with spring water spurting from an old drill hole at the side of the tunnel. Gizmo's excitement while playing under the water spout was cut short when Marco resumed walking.

Coming around the bend and through a straight stretch of tunnel, Marco noticed a faint ray of light coming from a distance. He maintained his gait, though completely baffled by the feeble light that broke through the dark underground chamber ahead of him. Believing it was a reflection of his light as it bounced off the wet tunnel floor, he turned off his flashlight. He then saw that the distant light was still there. Making a quick assessment of the source of the mysterious light creeping through, he realized it was coming from the surface. He pumped his fist in the air repeatedly in a burst of excitement. "Why didn't I think of that earlier?" he exclaimed, as he continued his brisk stride. He observed the light getting brighter as they closed in on it. "This could be the last stretch of our walk to freedom. The gleam of light appears to be an indication that an opening exists on a hillside."

Reminiscent of what he did at the entry portal, Marco broke a few decaying timber barricades and thrust his lanky body out to freedom, but not before he stashed the assault rifle underneath the rocks just inside the tunnel. "I suppose I don't have a need for an assault rifle anymore, and I don't want it to get into the wrong hands again."

There was sunlight left when they reached the surface. Enjoying the fresh air and staring at the portal, he said in amazement, "It looks so unreal to me that we actually went below ground through a portal on one side of the mountain and came out through the other."

He cautiously scouted the surrounding areas to make certain that the hills were free from devious men who displayed no qualm in shooting at people they perceived as a threat to their illegal trade.

Navigating the countryside with the aid of his compass, they reached Aladdin's location before nightfall. Seeking a suitable campsite before darkness set in, Marco rode farther north until he saw an excellent location. Less than two hundred meters below the trail, although not visible from it, a level area next to a brook would be the perfect site to pitch his tent.

At that point, it wasn't clear to him if his discovery of the vast source of narcotics was no longer an issue for the moment, or whether he was now in a dangerous situation. He was safe if the brutish drug traffickers believed that he was entombed in the tunnel. Or he could be tracked on the northbound trail if the gunmen realized that he might have escaped somehow through other tunnel breakthroughs to the surface, particularly if they found hoofprints unobliterated by the afternoon rains. Hereafter, he must watch his back with more vigilance.

That night, Marco tossed and turned in his tent. He couldn't believe that ruthless people existed in these grandiose mountains he truly cared about.

After breakfast, Marco bathed in the cold but clean and refreshing water flowing along the brook. He bathed Aladdin and Gizmo, too, after taking care of their needs.

He was set for a close encounter with the giant eagle.

CHAPTER 8
A DANGEROUS GAME

A loud, wing-flapping sound reverberated against the high rock wall, getting closer and closer, sending chills down his spine.

The team throttled back their pace a notch when Marco recognized the landmarks and found that they were getting close to the presumed eagle's domain.

"Whoa! Aladdin. Slow down, boy," he commanded his spirited mount while holding back the reins. "We're now near Mount Malvar. This must be very close to the spot where the eagle vanished from my sight several days ago, across the tall cliff above," he said, recalling the earlier incident with the predator. He hastily led his team down to a dry creek bed. They stopped at a spot he had chosen—an eroded gully under a clump of trees and shrubs facing the cliff at an angle.

As he dismounted, he heard wings flapping not far away. Seeking the source of the sound, he saw a huge eagle emerge from the cliff. It slightly changed course and then flew south.

"Despite its excellent eyesight, the eagle didn't see us. Is it possible that it ignored our presence here?" He placed the leash on Gizmo and tied the canine to a tree but decided against it at the last second. Having seen what the eagle could do to a grown monitor lizard, he realized that Gizmo, if tied to a tree, wouldn't stand a chance to protect himself against the predator. "I'll release my dog so he can run and protect himself in case the eagle attacks."

Marco relieved his horse of the bridle and kept it inside the utility bag. He tucked the stirrups and used Aladdin's short grazing rope to secure him to a peg he drove into the ground.

From his location, he realized that he was too far from the cliff to catch a glimpse of anything on the rock wall, much less discover an eagles' nest. With the use of his larga vista, he focused his sight on the same spot where he saw the predator take off, but he couldn't see anything there. He would need to move closer.

Running across the valley toward the cliff, Marco jumped into a shallow spillway midway between the gully and the rock wall. There, he discovered a near-level platform on the cliff that seemed deep enough to support an eagle's nest; maybe even a flock of giant eagles.

"What could that tangled heap on the platform be? Could that be an eagle's nest made up of twigs and dry leaves?" He had seen photographs of eagles' nests in one of his recently purchased books. There were pictures showing nests supported by crowns or sturdy branches of emergent trees in the rainforests, but none that were built on cliffs or ravines. This is amazing, he thought, while he continued to examine the nest laid out on the cliff ledge. "It may not look exactly the way it was depicted in the book, but it would still validate the concept that eagles possess outstanding parental virtues by building their nests in isolated, hard-to-reach places high above ground, which serves to keep their hatchlings safe from other predators."

Marco strapped his knapsack to his back and secured the bottom to his belt. The west-flank climb to the top of the cliff would be tough, but it was the only access to the peak without special climbing equipment. Led by his dog, their ascent of the lofty crag went better than he expected. At times he slid down the slippery portions of the slope while grasping Gizmo's collar and dragging the dog down with him. Hanging onto his pet, he joked, "We'll reach the top provided we climb ten steps for every slide we make." When they reached the top, he quickly laid on his stomach. He inspected the cliff in this prone position, as he often did for viewing or inspecting an outdoor scenery.

The vegetation cropping out from the fissures and voids on the cliff blocked his view. He couldn't see anything but the loose pieces of broken rocks and pebbles at the bottom of the rock wall. After moments of deep thought, he decided to scale the cliff. If he could descend several meters down the rock wall, he would be free of visual obstructions, and see what lay beneath the shrubbery and bushes below. He longed for a view of the nest he saw on the erosion-carved ledge of the cliff.

Marco descended slowly and carefully.

He regretted not bringing a longer rope to help him scale the cliff. "Well, that's my biggest mistake. Aladdin's grazing rope is not long enough to reach as far down as I intend to go. Besides, I needed that short rope to tie him down."

He was busy in his thoughts while he continued his slow descent. "A few meters more and I'll be atop the cluster of shrubs below. Then I'll go down to the next layer and stop there. I should be able to view the ledge from that point. If I can reach that far down without climbing aids, I can go up with little or no problem at all. In this case, ascending the cliff is much easier than descending it. I'll just have to take my time and be extra careful."

Marco thought he had a plan that could work in any typical situation. While he realized that things could go wrong at any time, he felt the rewards were well worth the risks he must take.

When he was a few meters below the top, he paused to ascertain whether his next foothold would be secure after transferring his hand support to the next group of shrubs.

Again, he heard the familiar squeals and the characteristic pitch inflections of the eagle. He knew that instant that the predator was soaring above. "The predator must have returned and spotted me on the cliff. I'm in trouble now. I hope it doesn't see my dog on the top of Mount Malvar."

He felt his heart pounding in his chest. The combination of excitement and his slight fear of the savage giant eagle were likely the reasons for the fast heartbeat.

The goal he had set for himself was simple and straightforward: establish a friendly alliance with the giant bird, and open possiblities to return for a real-world experience with it. He wanted to contribute in the eagle conservation program. He was thrilled with prospect, and why not? As a future biologist, he'd be involved in enhancing the survival of the threatened giant birds.

Easier said than done? Time would tell if his purpose and resolve would help him succeed in this endeavor.

Marco heard the high-pitched whistles again moments before the winged hunter of the Caraballo Mountains dove from the sky. A few seconds later, loud, wing-flapping sounds reverberated against the high rock wall, and they sounded closer and closer, sending chills down his spine.

He was on the cliff in a precarious spot, supported only by a clump of shrubs.

It didn't help that Marco's vision was momentarily impaired by the sun's glare. Squinting against it, he looked up to behold the shadowy form of the huge eagle pulling up from its dive while positioning its powerful claws to grab his knapsack from behind.

"Got to move out of the eagle's claws quickly and keep it off-target," he grunted as he reached to grasp a growth of shrubs on his right for support. He realized that he had just made a serious mistake he would soon regret. He over-reached. He was able to grasp the vegetation trunk firmly but in his haste to evade the eagle, his foot slipped. Having lost his foothold, he hung from the vegetation with his full weight. The clump was pulled off its roots.

He fell nearly eight meters down the cliff and landed on another layer of vegetation. The shrubs slowed down his fall, but his body passed through. The next layer of vegetation wasn't thick enough to stop his momentum and he went through again. Marco landed on a cluster of bushes that seemed sturdy enough to arrest his fall, but he broke and uprooted half of the shrubs. This caused him to lose his balance. He would have fallen farther down the cliff but he moved quickly enough to grab a thicker bunch of vegetation that was robust enough to support his weight.

Peering down the almost vertical rock wall, Marco realized that his feet were dangling above the ledge. He took the only option left for him.

With both hands grasping the vegetation for support, he turned his back to the rock wall and let go of his hold. He slid three meters or so down the cliff wall to the ledge below and landed on both feet. He found himself holding onto the huge nest to avoid falling off the ledge.

Marco sat next to the nest and let loose a loud cry of joy. He felt shock and disbelief as to how he got himself into such a dangerous situation and lived to reflect on it.

Enduring unspeakable pain from his battered body, he carefully examined his aching limbs to determine whether he had suffered broken bones, dislocations, or deep cuts. He was bleeding from scratches and lacerations over various parts of his body, including his mouth, face, and head. Happy to have survived, he expected to recover fully from his superficial injuries.

"The vegetation on the cliff saved me from certain death, thank God."

He took the anti-infection cream from his knapsack and

treated his open wounds.

In the midst of all that was going through his mind, Marco managed a smile while he gazed at the nest. "I presume the eagle has a mate and they are out hunting prey somewhere."

He intended to sit still on the ledge and mind his own business, hoping that the predator who had attacked him earlier would be calm again when it got back on the ledge with its prey. Marco would be ready, however, to protect himself in the event that he'd be attacked again.

Moments after the predator lunged at Marco and missed, it flew above the cliff and circled a few times above Gizmo before attacking the canine. The giant eagle and the German shepherd began their life-and-death battle atop Mount Malvar. The fierce struggle raged on with neither side gaining the upper hand. Gizmo fought valiantly as he always had in past scuffles with other animals. He gave all he could to stay out of the eagle's powerful claws and whenever he saw an opportunity, he snapped his fearsome jaws at the plucky predator.

The eagle was unable to pin down the scrappy dog because of his speed, evasiveness, and grit. It backed away and flew to a perch on a nearby tree branch.

The ensuing lull gave Gizmo the opportunity to descend to the base of the cliff via the west flank.

Though the fight between the spirited dog and the ferocious eagle was out of his sight, Marco had heard everything going on atop that cliff. After he had settled on the ledge, he envisioned how the battle was fought and who was gaining control. Listening intently while Gizmo was making a gallant stand against the eagle, he was comforted to know that the dog was snarling and yapping; not whimpering in submission. "From the sounds I hear, my dog seems to be fighting without fear to ward off the eagle's attacks."

"Good work, Gizmo. I'm so proud of you. Keep up the

good fight and save your hide," he whispered to himself as he sat on the ledge, tending his injuries. "I feel badly to have put you in this predicament, only to become unable to help you out of it."

Having regrouped for its next attack, the hungry eagle didn't waste much time on its perch. It renewed the savage aerial assault on the dog at the base of the cliff.

Gizmo ran in every direction to evade the eagle's sharp talons while he occasionally stopped and turned around to snarl, bare fangs, and fight back. He leapt a few times to attack the eagle, but the predator was quick to withdraw and keep its claws away from the dog's jaws.

Once he spotted Aladdin tethered to a peg on the gully, Gizmo ran and stayed close to the horse for protection. The eagle pounced on the dog while he was under the horse but the canine evaded the predator and stayed away from its deadly claws.

Troubled by the intense fight raging near his flanks and belly, Aladdin bolted and broke out of his tether.

Gizmo caught up and trotted alongside the galloping horse. The dog remained out of danger from the attacking eagle by staying close to Aladdin.

The giant eagle sensed the unwitting alliance between the two four-legged animals and flew away to its hunting range, perhaps in search of more favorably disposed prey to gratify its hunger.

Marco was meditative over which was more hazardous; falling off the cliff, or being snatched by the giant eagle. If he'd had foreknowledge of the extreme hazard of having no stable hand and foot support on the cliff, he might have allowed himself to be snatched up by the winged predator. After all, the eagle's predictable action at the time would be to drop him on the ledge if he had been caught. If the eagle attacked him there, he would have a fair chance of survival, knowing that he could better protect himself standing on a flat surface than by hanging precariously on the cliff. On a similar but more lethal note, however, the eagle could have grabbed and dropped him in mid-air to his death at the bottom of the cliff. However the cards were dealt, there was an inherent hazard involved that could have turned deadly, one way or the other. Much to his relief, he was still alive.

Calming his stunned and frazzled mind, Marco deflected the petrifying thoughts rushing through his brain back to his incredible fortune of having survived the perilous fall. He'd won a very dangerous game he hadn't planned on playing.

CHAPTER 9
EAGLES' LEDGE

How long can I survive without food and water until my family or friends find me? Can I co-exist with the eagles until I'm rescued?

Marco sat quietly by the gaping ledge on the cliff, consumed in thoughts of his hair-raising experience. Despite suffering from severe pains over his body, he was able to inspect both sides of the cliff to find that there was no safe way out. He was stunned when he realized that without a rope or other rock climbing equipment, he had nowhere to go. He had become a captive on the ledge.

The huge nest was constructed from twigs and leaves. Inaccessible from the top or the bottom of the cliff, he estimated that the nest was built on top of a platform three meters wide by one and a half meters deep. It was about seventy-five meters above the foot of the cliff, and thirty-five meters below the top of the towering structure.

A myriad of questions relevant to his survival and early escape from the ledge raced through his mind. Among these were: How long can I subsist without food and water until my family or friends find me? Can I co-exist with the eagles until I'm rescued? Can I find a way to scale the nearly vertical cliff to get out of the ledge? Can Aladdin and Gizmo find their way home and alert my family that I needed help on the ledge?

Although there could be no immediate resolutions to these

troubling questions, he hoped he would find answers before long.

The key to his survival was to have continued access to food. He would set up a simple water recovery system for his water needs. He assumed he had enough food in his pockets and knapsack to last for several days. He took an inventory to make certain that he had enough food to last him until he could plan for a safe way out from the cliff.

He had water in his canteen, a large bag of peanuts, and some preserved and canned foods inside his knapsack. These would last from five days to one week if he ate less than he would normally consume. The canned foods and uncooked rice tied to the back of his saddle were no longer available.

He had his Swiss army knife, light plastic raincoat, flashlight and batteries, and a spool of cotton twine that had helped him bundle his things and pitch his tent. Extra T-shirts, underwear, and a bamboo flute were also packed inside his knapsack. He found two boxes of matches wrapped in plastic, and a light-duty compass: necessary items for mountain treks, but not much use on the ledge.

Holding the bamboo flute Amanda gave him before he rode out, he tried to recall what the retired wildlife photographer had told his mother when she interviewed him for her term paper many years ago. He couldn't remember the exact words the former had told his mother, but it sounded like he used the wind gadget to tame and calm the eagles before he took pictures of them. "He played the flute to calm the eagles?"

Marco made a concerted effort to learn how to generate shrill sounds using the flute. He blew across the hole near the closed end of the tube and experimented on which of the six holes to block, searching for the combination of holes that would produce the appropriate high-pitched sounds that could catch the attention of the eagles. Charming the predator was a real challenge, and it stood to reason that he must make it his goal or at least come very close to what Mr. Madera was able to pull off.

But more than ever, he must find a way to get off the ledge, and fast. He did not have a single clue on how to survive the eagle's ledge when his stocked food was consumed.

His thoughts were cut short when loud rustles from huge wings marked the arrival of the eagle as it landed on the ledge with a prey, a brown, long-tailed Philippine monkey.

Marco looked straight ahead, avoiding eye contact with the predator, and followed its every movement with his peripheral vision. He exercised extreme caution in not agitating, provoking, or drawing undue attention from the hungry predator, who had begun to feed on its prey. *"It seems strange for the winged predator not to notice my presence here. Maybe the eagle's just too hungry to notice anything at all."*

Closely observing the threatening sky, he saw brilliant flashes across the horizon. Then, as thunder echoed its deep-toned rumbles across the mountains, the scent of rain vaporizing on the sunbaked earth filled the air.

The downpour began in earnest thereafter, and when he reached for his plastic raincoat inside his knapsack that was resting against the cliff, he discovered that moving closer to the rock wall kept him dry. The leafy canopy above protected him and the eagle from the rain.

Thankfully, the summer wind wasn't blowing against the cliff, or else he and the eagle would be caught dripping wet in the heavy downpour.

His mind strayed a bit as he wished he had a weathervane on the side of the cliff to show him which way the rain would be directed, toward or away from the cliff wall.

Using rocks, twigs, and his plastic raincoat, he devised a

way to collect and save rainwater for drinking. He could later improve his "rainwater recovery system" if he remained on the ledge longer than he expected.

"Save money for the rainy days" was an old adage he'd learned in school. In this case, "Save water for the dry spell" rang true. The dry spell, however, wouldn't be around until six or seven months later. Indeed, Marco was lucky to have the seasonal downpours providing him water for drinking and washing. Excessive rain may have a handful of downsides, but water has its reasons for being.

Marco's supply of drinking water should be ample, no doubt, because as the rainy season was in close association with the warm summer months, afternoon precipitations were becoming regular.

He was proud of his improvised drinking water recovery system.

How about his food after his stocked supply was gone? Would he be able to eat dried raw meat if the eagles allowed him to take his share? What choice of prey do the big birds have? He couldn't be picky in as much as his food supply would be limited only to what the eagles hunted and brought to the ledge.

Marco knew the predators were more likely to hunt monkeys, other birds of prey, reptiles, bats, squirrels, and rabbits in their vast hunting range. A Philippine brown deer might fall prey to the giant predators, but only on rare occasions.

"I must address the food issues now rather than later, and adapt to my new environment."

In years past, Amanda dried salted pork and stored it in jars while Marco watched. She explained to him that preserving meat was a good alternative to storing it in their compact freezer compartment. When they butchered pigs on the farm for their consumption, she stocked the excess salted pork for preservation.

What did it portend? It fortified Marco's mind-set that survival on the ledge was possible. As long as the eagle provided him a share of the prey, albeit in limited quantity, Marco could process palatable portions by drying them out in the sun. If he were to make a choice between starving and eating sundried, choice meat parts, he'd pick the latter.

Watching the eagle constantly hunt prey to feed itself, his everyday food supply seemed assured, although it would come to one judicious question; would he be able to get a share of the prey?

Marco was startled when another eagle landed on the ledge. The newcomer appeared slightly smaller than the other eagle, but was equally imposing and fearsome. He guessed that the newly landed predator was the male partner.

"He must be very hungry," Marco observed, as the predator immediately began to tear away at what was left of his mate's prey.

He had read that eagles are like gorillas; they mate for life. One seeks another mate only when the previous one dies.

Contrary to what he had previously suspected, the eagles did not bother him at all. The twigs and leaves that constituted most parts of their nest nearly separated him from the big birds.

Marco was pleased with what he saw. "With an extra big mouth to feed, two hunters are better than one."

He learned that when there was a need for providing food and protecting their young from rain and other natural elements, the male eagle was known to deliver his equal share of the responsibilities. Inequity was found to take place only during the incubation period. The female predator spent more than half of her time hatching the egg through the day, but as nighttime fell, she was willed to do all the incubating work.

Often, the predators incubated one egg at a time, but on rare occasions, they incubated two eggs simultaneously.

Discreetly watching the nest, Marco hadn't heard nor seen a hatchling on the nest; nor an egg still in incubation. Upon closer inspection, he spotted a broken eggshell lying inside the nest. "The eagles must have produced a barren egg in their latest reproductive cycle."

Eagle mates share the care of their young. With an empty nest, they might find no reason to stay on the ledge longer than necessary.

Observing the monkey-eating eagles with keen interest, Marco's face brightened with a smile when he noticed how accurate his mother had described the predators to him. "She depicted them to a tee, except for their actual extraordinary size. She made her research on the eagles in high school, with attention to details, and by asking people who had been involved with them. Once you set your eyes on their remarkable features, they give you enough reasons to help them survive. They captivate you for life. Mama will be very eager to hear more about them, especially with respect to their size."

He'd learned from his mother that the species is indigenous to the Philippines. The islands have always stood alone, and were never linked to or found to have drifted away from a larger land mass. No monkey-eating eagle was found to exist in other countries.

At the cliff ledge whereupon he spent his first night with the giant eagles, he experienced the strangest feeling of co-existing with the wild predators. He might not be quite familiar with them, but they certainly captured his attention.

While he couldn't sleep during his first night on the hard, uneven platform, Marco was determined not to let it break his spirit.

Pulling a twig from the nest, he sharpened both ends to

protect himself from the predators in the event he were attacked.

He was alert until the morning hours, holding the twig and his Swiss army knife in each hand. So far, at any time during his entrapment, there was no sign that an attack by the eagles was imminent. The thought of living with them for an indefinite period of time kept him awake all night. "This concern has to be addressed now." Laying his "weapons" aside, he stood up and moved toward the predators.

The eagles stared at him; their manes erect as they sensed a confronting action from an intruder. The eagles moved to protect their space on the ledge.

Watching the eagles' subsequent actions, Marco was convinced that the giant predators were indeed belligerent, making him more apprehensive. He knew that he could be attacked at any time. As heedless as he could be at times, he took a step toward the huge nest and crouched over to touch the eagles; a risky bid that might possibly serve as a precursor to the taming and subjugation of the species if a positive response was shown. They made high-pitched sounds, and quickly stepped in to block Marco from encroaching farther into their corner. The eagles were poised to defend their space at all costs, and appeared ready to attack if he made one more move. He was in a bind.

"What will I do if they jump me? I can hurt them, but they can hurt me, too, or kill me if they are relentless in their attack. They have the advantage of their ability to hover overhead and attack me time after time with their sharp claws and beaks. They could knock me off the ledge. I don't want to kill or maim them, or face the risk of injury or death."

He backed away from the eagles and sat down on the ledge. "What will I do next?" he pondered.

From his readings and his recent experiences with the predators, Marco learned that monkey-eating eagles are merciless when they attack their prey, whether on the ground or while soaring above. And they are known to be super-strong. They can kill and carry off large prey such as goats, pigs, dogs, and even brown deer.

The male eagle flew from the nest. He swooped from the ledge in a steep dive, demonstrating his swiftness and agility. Flying alone, perhaps aware that his mate was watching, he showcased an aerial display of what was part of the pair's flying repertoire. Marco had no idea how close the eagles were to mating, taking into consideration the lengthy two-year period between gestations.

The predator leveled off and soared into the rising sun until he was out of Marco's sight. "That was quite a show."

In spite of their excellent hunting skills and tenacity, eagles have been found to have less than eighty percent success in bagging their prey. He wished the male predator, who went out in search of food, total success in the hunt. He hoped the eagle would bring a rabbit or monkey to the ledge, his preferred meat.

When the female eagle settled down, Marco attempted to mend their relationship. He began his act by sounding off his wind gadget, creating a series of high-pitched whistles that seemed to mimic the shrill sounds produced by the giant eagles. He hoped that he could duplicate the success of Mr. Madera in drawing the predators' attention to the point of charming them, as he had alleged. He was persistent in carrying out this task, pausing only to rest and observe the reaction of the lone eagle.

For the second time in as many days, he crouched over to the nest and tried to touch the eagle. Surprisingly, she didn't show signs of hostility or her vaunted fierceness. He noted her sharp stare, but this time it appeared more restrained. Marco sensed that something enthusing and central to his goal was stirring up. Keeping an eye on the eagle, he seized the moment after he had detected an opening. He touched her, offering assurances by way of words, whispers, and gestures that his only intent was to develop a real friendship amongst themselves as they continued to live together on the ledge. In his usual gentle tones, he continued, "I'm not here to encroach on your home. And don't think that I'll be here for long," he said, not expecting the eagle to understand a single word he uttered.

Standing motionless, the female eagle continued to stare at Marco with her piercing blue-gray eyes. Suddenly, she spread her enormous wings and ambled toward him in an apparent acceptance of the friendship he was offering. He made an effort to touch the eagle's white and brown plumage, moving his hand upward to soothe her disheveled crest that resembled a lion's mane. He was careful to avoid sudden or unnecessary movement that could be misconstrued as confrontational. He continued to caress the eagle's nape for as long as she allowed him, gazing at the eagle's prominent, bluish-gray beak she used to tear her prey apart.

Several years ago, when he and his family moved from the mine to their farm home, Marco was given a pet chicken as a gift from friends.

He recalled the day the chicken, named Dixie, was about to be grabbed by a hungry hawk. Marco arrived at the scene of the attack, without a full second to spare, and thwarted the assault. Every time he took the chicken out of her pen, she followed him around the yard with her wings spread.

Amanda interpreted the gesture as the pet's way of asking for affection from her master. Marco simply took it as her way of cuddling her master.

He would learn in the coming days that his involvement with his pet chicken, and later with the eagles, paralleled in many ways. He correlated the past and present experiences, practiced his findings, and enriched his rapport with the winged predators.

Delighted with the preceding events and with lifted spirits, he smiled for the first time in many days in anticipation of better things to come. He expected to befriend the male eagle when he returned from his hunt, just like he had with his partner. He was very much aware that his survival on the ledge depended on his success in building a strong relationship with the eagles.

Despite living on the edge of the cliff as an accidental captive of the winged predators, and bereft of life's basic needs, he remained as healthy as he could expect. For this reason, he constantly expressed his thanks to God and entreated his blessings to be reunited with his family.

"Mistakes happen. The past is gone. It's what comes next that counts now."

CHAPTER 10

ENTRAPPED

Fourteen of my men are entombed. Fourteen lives are in peril.
We'll do everything to get them out alive, and we won't fail ...

Olin Vega was the day shift supervisor at the 150ML (150 meter level) main tunnel on a stormy period in July 1970. A tropical rainstorm alternating with heavy monsoon rains battered the area for many weeks. The downpour had been quite heavy the night before, creating a run-off that cascaded down the Simla Creek with such force that it threatened the destruction of everything in its path. It wasn't possible to cross it.

Olin and his crew had to find a way to cross the raging creek, their only access to the tunnel portal on the other side of the mountain. The miners needed to enter the portal and walk into the depths of the tunnel to get to their workplace—the underground mine.

To reach their bunk quarters, the outgoing graveyard shift crew had to get across to the opposite bank.

Olin and the crews on either side of the swollen creek strung a cable line across the flow and anchored the ends to trees on both sides. The men took turns crossing the Simla Creek by grasping the taut cable, hands alternately sliding forward until the opposite banks were reached safely.

The last miner to cross the creek slipped from his hold of the cable and fell into the water. The powerful current dragged him downstream. Luckily, he was able to hold onto a huge boulder for a few seconds while quick action by Olin and the others saved him from certain death.

The men formed a human chain, each one holding the belt of the person ahead of him. The last one anchored himself to the cable while Olin, the front man, pulled the miner out of the water to safety.

Olin and his day crew were dripping wet, despite their raincoats. It was cold, and the wind chill made it even worse. To ease the problem to some extent, the shivering men ran to the compressor shed to stay out of the wind and the rain. "Start the compressor," Olin said to one of his men who knew how to operate such machinery. "Compressed air and heat generated by the diesel engine can dry our clothes fast."

When the rains abated and the water flow diminished, construction crews built a reinforced concrete bridge across the creek. From then on, the crews crossed in any weather.

Olin was asked to report to Rick Gannon, the mine manager. He was pulling up a chair when Amadeo Brown, the assistant mine manager, walked into Rick's office.

"Good morning, Mr. Gannon, and you too, Mr. Brown," Olin said.

"Good morning, Olin."

"Gentlemen," the mine manager said, "I called you here this morning to remind you of our commitment to the expansion program, which is tied to the development of our Lone Branch Orebodies. As we had discussed earlier, tonnages for our production expansion would be provided by the lower-level orebodies. We will continue driving the 150ML main tunnel as our access to the Lone Branch, and eventually, as our ventilation and drainage conduits. To keep you reminded, I mentioned our expansion program, although it's not part of our agenda today."

"Olin, you were highly recommended by Mr. Brown to be in charge of the underground project, and other related work at the Long Branch Levels," Rick said after a brief pause. "As such, you will supervise three shift crews and will report to Mr. Brown and myself. Your promotion as a Mine Development Foreman will be on an acting capacity and will be confirmed after a sixty-day probationary period."

Pleased with his upcoming promotion, he thanked the mine executives for giving him the opportunity to earn a bigger role in his service to the company.

If my promotion deserves a celebration, I'll get my family involved, and that may happen on my next visit home, Olin decided.

"Mr. Brown will take you to the Personnel Department. They will explain to you the benefits commensurate to such a position. Later, he will take you to his office and explain the pay plan, what the job entails, and what your responsibilities will be. Any questions, gentlemen?"

He thanked Amadeo and Olin and adjourned the conference after Olin chose to save any questions he may have for their next meeting.

Months later, confirmed as Mine Development Foreman, Olin prepared to walk through the three-kilometer 150ML tunnel to oversee his men working underground. As had been his daily routine, he went in after checking the reports of supervisors who had worked the swing and graveyard shifts.

The report from the graveyard shift supervisor indicated that there was a drastic increase in water flow from the main shaft during the night. Olin noticed that the rail track was almost submerged in water.

The crew must have cut through an aquifer, releasing a large volume of water, or they could have tapped a major fissure from upstream Ural Creek, he thought.

He waded in water in the deeper parts of the tunnel until he reached the underground workings. He conferred with his men about the flooding on the tunnel floor. "Did we encounter a big gush of water anywhere?" Olin asked his shift supervisor, Kobi.

"I saw minor water seepages this morning, but I suppose those weren't the problem. Water splashing down the main shaft was causing the flooding of the tunnel floor. I couldn't determine where it's coming from," Kobi said.

"Come with me. Let's make the rounds together."

Olin and Kobi climbed the main shaft, taking the staggered wooden ladder stairway instead of using the compressed air-operated Alimak raise climber. "I haven't used the wooden stairway for months," Olin said. "It will be good to inspect it on our way up."

A significant volume of water splattered down the shaft like a miniature waterfall. It was a cause of concern but it didn't deter them; they continued to climb the staggered ladders like the plucky miners they were.

When they reached the access tunnel platform connecting the main to the auxiliary shaft, they saw the tunnel crew just pulling out from their workplace.

"Weak rock has been freshly exposed, and excessive water seepages made our work dangerous due to the high probability of tunnel collapse," the lead miner told Olin and Kobi. "The sudden appearance of crumbling rock needs extensive ground support before work can be resumed. I decided to withdraw my crew from the shaft and assigned them to bring in timber supports from the portal area."

What caught Olin's attention, and perhaps even more disconcerting than the excessive water inflow, was the composition of the water discharge. It was turbid, and very similar to surface run-off during heavy rains.

"The critical issues that we need to address are the support of newly exposed weak ground and the potential for a large onrush of water from the surface," Olin said.

"That's my assessment, too," Kobi agreed.

"Then let's get to work right now, this very minute."

"As a safety measure, I'd like to suggest that the ventilation door on the shaft connecting the tunnel be reinforced and converted into a heavy bulkhead," Kobi said. "It will retain its function as a ventilation door, but it must be reinforced to serve as a safety partition as well."

"I can see your good point there. In the event that the main shaft collapses, water and debris would flood the mine workings at the main tunnel level. We—all of us, including the tunnel crews below—can seek higher ground here. The reinforced bulkhead will stop or at least slow down the onrush of water and debris through the main shaft," Olin concurred.

"That's exactly my point, boss," Kobi said.

"Assign the lead miner and his crew to do the job immediately. The incoming swing crew can bring in more material and timber support. Provide him with additional men if necessary, even if you have to suspend work in other areas," he said.

Olin reported to Amadeo Brown in the latter's office that afternoon.

He provided him with an update of activities involving the 150ML main tunnel, the shafts, and other work areas.

"Mr. Brown, I have reason to believe that the main shaft could fail at the top with catastrophic results, unless safety measures such as control of excessive water seepage from the surface and shoring of weak ground are implemented immediately. We have sped up the propping of weak areas, but the excessive water problem has to be assessed and implemented by a higher authority, as it could involve the use of heavy equipment."

"I acknowledge your assessment of the situation in your area. Rest assured, however, that the shaft will not fail on its own, because we blasted through solid rock in most areas, and the weak sections were adequately shored up either with timber, concrete, or roof bolts," Amadeo said.

He acknowledged Olin's assessment of the situation, but he didn't provide a solution to the problem. Olin didn't think he understood his argument. "The shaft is not in danger of collapsing at any time, but run-off materials from the surface could be dumped through the opening and plug the shaft. If that happens, we could be facing untold problems underground."

"You can count on my word that we'll look into that."

Olin left the office of the boss with the vestige of a possible shaft blowout and the prospect of prolonged and costly downtime, not factoring in the potential hazards that the men would be faced with.

Amadeo went to see Rick Gannon in his office. They talked about the main operations briefly, but discussed the 150ML tunnel situation at length. Rick asked him about Olin, and how he was handling the problems down there. "Olin is a very capable manager, who leads by example. He can motivate his men and get their full support at all times. His decisions are sound."

Two days later, a loud and frightening roar was heard by the miners underground. Water, silt, and rocks careened down the deep and dark main shaft into the main tunnel, one hundred meters below the top of the shaft. A powerful air blast followed within seconds and was felt everywhere, including the portal area.

Mechanical maintenance technicians at the tunnel portal felt the air blast. They were alarmed. They informed the miners at the portal who were just about to walk into the tunnel to start their shift.

The shaft blowout was recorded at two thirty-five in the afternoon. Olin and Kobi were inspecting the newly reinforced bulkhead at the access tunnel between the shafts at precisely that time. They heard a loud roar that miners dread to hear— the sound of watery debris from surface run-off as materials were squeezed through the underground openings by the force of gravity. Entrapment resulted when the access openings were plugged by water and debris. The roar was followed by a heavy pounding noise against the bulkhead; thump after thump. The bulkhead was partially damaged on one side when the angled buttress support split, but it remained intact after Olin and

Kobi braced it. Water and silt gushed through the seams, but the bulkhead withstood the battering.

Olin and his miners walked away to survey the damage and check on the rest of the crews. They were more than halfway down the auxiliary shaft when they noticed that there were men ascending.

"Who's down there?"

"The tunnel crews," several voices shot back.

Dante, one of the lead miners assigned to work in one of the tunnels, spoke for the group. "We heard the frightening roar and we knew that something serious happened. Two crews, including mine, sprinted away from the tunnel face toward the 150ML tunnel."

"What about the third crew? Where were they when you reached the 150ML tunnel?" Olin asked.

"We didn't see them there. They were probably loading timbers outside at the portal area at the time of the blowout," Dante said. "Water and debris were coming down from the main shaft and filling the main tunnel. Water was rising to the roof so fast and, to avoid drowning, both crews scrambled to higher ground by ascending the auxiliary shaft."

Olin ordered his men to continue climbing the auxiliary shaft and wait for help at the access tunnel. "It's the safest retreat area I know of right now, and we can organize and make plans there."

There was no possible means of communication between the workers on the surface and the men trapped underground.

A technician tried to operate the phone in order to call management at main operations, but there was no dial tone. Linemen had been working on the line earlier, and it was obvious that they hadn't resolved the problem.

The lead technician, Nardo, grabbed the closed circuit,

single-band radio that Olin used as a backup when the phone was not working or when he was away from his office. He called main operations, and was delighted to get a crackling answer.

"You're coming in broken. Please move away from any signal obstruction, over." It was Brown who answered. He had been driving, but stopped in a clear area to receive a better signal. "This is Amadeo Brown, do you read me? Over."

"I read you loud and clear. Please drive immediately to the 150ML tunnel. There is a serious problem here. Over."

"What's the problem? Over."

"I don't know exactly what it is but I think it's serious, and I suggest you come here as soon as you can. Over."

"Okay, I'm on my way there. Over and out."

Brown wondered why the water was brown with silt. Where is the mud coming from? He decided to investigate the shaft opening at the surface. "Let's go and check where this water is coming from," he said to Mario, one of the idle swing shift miners waiting to be reassigned to another place of work.

He drove his CJ-5 Renegade Jeep five kilometers uphill until he reached a fork on the road. He took the split on the right that led to an area previously levelled by a bulldozer. He pointed out to Mario the site of the shaft collar as he recalled it. "It should be right around here. Wait a second, Mario; where is the shaft?"

They were appalled to see a river of rock and mud instead of the shaft collar. The whole area, including the shaft opening, was covered with several hundred tons of mud and debris. Walking upstream, Amadeo suspected that water may have diverted toward the shaft collar site because of a drastic decrease in the flow along the Ural Creek. As they went farther up, they heard the sound of a small waterfall.

Their investigation steered them to a big landslide that

blocked the flow of storm water on the Ural Creek, causing a major backup. The rising water on the newly-formed dam eroded an embankment as water, laden with gravel and silt, cascaded down the hillside and found its way into the shaft opening.

Amadeo radioed Rick Gannon to send a D7 Caterpillar bulldozer to the shaft collar site right away. "I'll wait for the equipment to arrive so I can direct the tractor operator to divert the flow of water away from the main shaft," he said.

Rick Gannon was on his way to visit the shaft collar and Ural Creek in order to confer with Amadeo Brown, and to determine the best way to solve the problem.

The plan was to prioritize the removal of the landslide blockage on the creek to keep the storm run-off flow unimpeded. This would stop the flow of water into the shaft. The shaft collar site would then be cleaned with debris.

Upon reaching the access tunnel from the auxiliary shaft, the men trapped underground: Olin, Kobi, and the twelve miners, sat down to rest. Ascending the shaft without resting was quite strenuous.

Kobi ordered the men to gather all the leftover boards and pieces of wood that were not used in the reinforcement of the bulkhead. The boards were laid horizontally on the tunnel floor so they could be used for resting and sleeping.

"Men, we are all aware of our entrapment underground," Olin spoke to his group. "Our two escape routes, the main shaft and the main tunnel, are blocked with tons of mud, water, and debris. I don't know when we will be able to walk out of here, but this I'm certain of; outside, as we speak, scores of able and hardworking men would be laboring around the clock to get us out of here. Let us keep our hopes high, for ourselves and for our families. We are miners: strong, tough, and resilient. We will make it out of here alive."

The trapped men were in good spirits. They had no food but had an unlimited supply of underground spring water. "We have plenty of water to drink. Big deal," Tomas clowned. He was the life of the party, dishing out jokes when he noticed that the men were quiet and deep in their thoughts.

In desperate times, such as an entrapment of men in an underground workplace, leadership of the group was appointed from the ranks, due to the absence of an assigned leader. In this case it was not necessary. Olin was there to lead his men.

Despite his mounting hunger and weakness, he continued to deliver motivational words to his men. "Stay with me, guys, and don't ever quit on me. Together, we will go through this difficult period. Be mindful that Northern Consolidated Copper Mines has all the necessary resources and the capability to get us out of here in short order."

Amanda and the boys occupied Olin's thoughts. *I hope the family recognizes the fact that I have the moral obligation to get through this tough ordeal and stay alive for them.*

He wondered when he would see her again.

That caused him to recollect an important event that changed his life many years ago. He was a miner, slated for promotion as a shift supervisor, when he met seventeen-year-old Amanda in the town market of San Antonio.

She was a popular high school senior with brains that matched her good looks, so to speak. A charming and dynamic young lady, she helped her parents sell vegetables and other farm crops at their stall every Sunday after church service.

Olin and his friends were looking for fruits and vegetables to buy at the marketplace when he saw Amanda helping a customer across the aisle. He quickly strode to Amanda's stall.

"Hi, I'm Olin. My friends and I are looking for fresh vegetables and fruits to bring home to our quarters in the mine."

"My name's Amanda. We have freshly harvested vegetables that you and your friends might be interested in. Look around while I help this other customer. I'll be with you shortly."

She came back a few moments later. "Thanks for waiting. What kind of vegetables are you looking for?" she asked.

"Potatoes, onions, green vegetables, broccoli, and cauliflower. A week's supply for myself. I see that you don't sell fruits here. Aside from the vegetables, I'd like to bring home a bag of fruits."

"For just yourself?"

"I live alone in my quarters in the mine."

"Oh! Pardon me, but I didn't mean to be snoopy."

"That's perfectly all right. Do you work here regularly?"

"Just Sundays—to assist my parents. I'm a senior at the St. Benedict Catholic High School. By the way, the lady with the blue apron three stalls away sells fresh fruits. Her name is Mira, and she can help you."

Olin and his friends boarded the bus bound for the mine with their bags full of fruits and vegetables. He was quiet for most of the seventy-five-minute trip; his thoughts were filled by the lovely Amanda.

Once more, he wondered when he would see her again.

To expedite work in the area, Rick and Amadeo decided to employ more equipment. Rick radioed Arthur Holly, the resident manager, to send a second Cat D7 bulldozer, and one Allis Chalmers 745 front-end loader to the area.

By mid-afternoon, the obstruction along the Ural Creek was almost removed. Clean up operations continued. Water resumed its normal flow along the creek. As the waterfall dried up, so did the shaft collar area.

Meanwhile, the portal area was buzzing with various activities: carpenter crews were erecting temporary personnel and equipment sheds in case of rain, electricians were installing power outlets at the portal and in the tunnel, pipe men and welders completed the installation of compressed air valves and underground outlets, trucks unloaded materials and equipment from the main operations, and food and water were being supplied to the rescue workers.

For safety reasons, the aggressive News Media Corporation reporters were advised by security not to stray too close to the area. The San Antonio Weekly Gazette personnel waited at a distance from the busy areas.

"Fourteen of my men are entombed. Fourteen lives are in peril. We'll do everything to get them out alive, and we won't fail," Rick Gannon said, assessing the daunting task ahead.

Amanda, Toby, and Marco visited the portal area, and like all other family members and friends of the trapped men, they were advised to wait for news at the main operations waiting room.

Extremely worried about their father, Marco and Toby obliged only after Amanda was promised by the mine spokesman to be provided with frequent updates of the rescue operation.

The drilling of two holes, twenty-five meters deep, from the surface to the access tunnel, was underway. When finished, the eight-centimeter diameter hole would provide an access to food for the men trapped below. Communication equipment would be lowered next.

A pneumatic (compressed-air operated) shovel-loader was employed to clean up debris from the tunnel. The shovel-loader scooped material from the tunnel floor and dumped it into three-ton cars.

A ten-car train, in tandem with a battery locomotive, continually unloaded the debris at a dumping station near the tunnel portal. An electric scraper equipped with a special bucket, and mounted on a raised flat car, was used to loosen and pull materials when possible.

Olin Vega and his men were getting weaker and emaciated but were still in good spirits. Their hopes of a speedy rescue were revived by the sound of the drilling above as the diamond cutting bit penetrated deeper into their location. They tried to conserve their strength by sleeping and minimizing their movements, but the vibration caused by the big drill rod kept them awake and excited.

Amadeo radioed Rick to suspend pulling out debris material from the 150ML main tunnel. The shaft was emptied down to twenty-eight meters, their pre-determined target depth. The plan was not to empty the shaft until all the men were rescued, as they would need a platform to work on during the rescue operation. The blocked access tunnel where the trapped men were expected to be rescued from was cleared from debris.

They decided to discontinue drilling the service holes as well. "That won't be necessary after all," Rick said. "The drilling crews, however, will remain on standby at their post until ordered to pull out or resume drilling."

After scaling the shaft walls of loose rocks, two trained mine rescuers, part of a team sent to rescue the trapped men, stepped into the hooded cage and went down and up a few times to test the system.

Satisfied that everything worked as expected, the rescuers were lowered to the access tunnel level. They secured the cage and entered the tunnel. The rescue crew pushed aside some of the rocks and debris on the tunnel floor to facilitate the movement of men during the rescue process.

They pried loose a few bulkhead boards and were able to reach the trapped men. Half of the men screamed with joy. The rest were too weak to be mobile, but were smiling and gesturing to thank the rescuers for their deliverance.

After eating soft food, soup, and other specially prepared food, the men gradually regained some of their strength and were able to stand and walk slowly.

Olin and Joaquin, one of the trained mine rescuers, recognized each other. He was the miner Olin, and his crew had saved from drowning at Simla Creek several months earlier. Joaquin recalled that it was Olin who pulled him out of the raging creek.

"Olin, let me repeat what I said during the safety and post-accident review meeting after the creek incident. Thank you all for saving my life. After the Simla Creek incident, I asked to be trained to become a member of the Mine Rescue Team to help my fellow workers in similar situations. If there's one moment to spare just so I can give back to my rescuers at Simla Creek, it is now," Joaquin said.

"Thank you for risking your lives to save ours. Thanks to you both, and the entire Mine Rescue Team," Olin said.

He told the rescuers that most of the men should be able to walk on their own to the cage. Four needed to be carried out on stretchers. The rescue team, however, decided to carry all fourteen men, including Olin, to the cage, and thence to the ambulance on stretchers.

The rescued men were met at the surface shaft opening by their families and friends, and by the mine management.

Art Holly was the first to greet them. Amanda, Toby, and Marco were on hand to smother Olin, who was overwhelmed with joy as his distressing experience was behind him and he was with his family again.

They had been trapped underground for five days and two hours.

All crew members on that day shift, except the three men thought to be outside the tunnel loading timbers before the blowout, were transported immediately to the infirmary, and then sent to the San Antonio General Hospital to undergo a thorough medical checkup and any necessary care. The three men that were missing were found dead at their workplace when the main tunnel debris was cleared, the timber supports still loaded on their flatcar.

Olin went through another flashback of his challenging but fulfilling twenty-seven years with the Northern Consolidated Copper Mines. He was in deep thoughts of the events surrounding the underground disaster. The mandatory medical checkup and medical care given at the hospital came last in his recollection. Again, he wondered why the three men who lost their lives were not able to make it to the shaft to escape the onrush of water and mud. "Well, fussing about the accident won't bring them back. I'll leave their story for others to look into and have them apprise me of the facts one day. I must know what really happened down there."

He snapped back to the present when he heard a loud knock at his door.

In retrospect of his years with the mining firm, Olin knew that he gave all he could for the only employer he ever had. In return, the company provided a level playing field for him to compete for the one available position in middle management. The job was handed to him hands-down.

He became nostalgic about the years he'd spent with the company because he felt that his days in mining were drawing to a close. Now he looked at farming as a beacon of opportunity, and a goal to accomplish while he and Amanda were still in the prime of their years.

Faced with compelling life-changing issues, he had to make a decision whether to remain on his job in the mine, leaving Amanda to accomplish most of the farm work, or leave his employment in order to help expand their farm business.

After going through a stagnant period, there were positive indications that the vegetable and crop industry was at the threshold of a breakout year. Olin wanted to make sure that he would make the right decision when the time came. He was at a crossroads. He could take one path or the other, but he had to choose one.

He heard another knock at his door, followed by Amanda's voice.

When he opened the door, Olin noticed that she was deeply

worried about something. He could read in her eyes that she had unpleasant news to convey.

"Come in, Amanda. What brought you here at this time of the night?" Olin gave her a peck on her cheek. "Have a seat. You look worried about something. What's bothering you?"

"Marco's been missing for ten days now. He took Aladdin and Gizmo for a trail ride in the mountains and didn't come home in four to five days as he said he would."

"Did you talk to Toby about it?" He held his wife's trembling hands to calm her down.

"Toby's not home. He left town to help Reggie fix his leaking roof. I sent Rosie to town to inform him that his brother had not returned since he took a trek to the mountains."

"I'll go and ask Mr. Brown to grant me an emergency leave of absence. Stay here. I'll be right back, and then we'll go home and plan what to do," Olin said.

CHAPTER 11

THE SEARCH FOR MARCO

While they waited for the rain to stop, Olin and Toby walked through the flora under the dense canopy, observing the diverse wildlife and the natural beauty of the tropical rainforest. They noted that it was vegetated with hundreds or more plants of different varieties from the ground to the top.

Olin and Amanda arrived home at close to midnight. Toby stood up and unlocked the door for them when he heard their footsteps on the front porch.

A sad aura engulfed the couple as they entered Marco's bedroom. They felt the painful reality that he wasn't coming home that night as soon as they were inside his bedroom. There was a strange stillness as Olin gazed up through the window into the dark and starless sky, seeking answers that neither he nor Amanda could provide.

Toby noticed the eerie silence and broke it. "Mom and Dad, I understand how you both feel. In my heart, I know that Marco is safe and well. His uncharacteristic failure to come home is quite unsettling, but I truly believe that he went camping with friends he met on the mountains.

Please stop worrying. He'll be fine."

"What shall we do now?" Amanda said.

"Start the search for Marco," Olin decided.

"Tonight?"

"Yes, we'll start our search tonight. Since we won't be able to sleep worrying about him, we might as well make use of the time allotted for sleeping," Olin said.

They packed some food, water, and other items they deemed necessary for the night search. "These two Koehler rechargeable miner's lamps I borrowed from the mine should come in handy," Olin said. "The recharging device came with the lamps, too."

"Good thing you told me that because I was going to ask how they would be recharged."

"Think positive, and expect good news about Marco," Olin said to Amanda. "Sleep as much as you can, because we have long days ahead of us. If you can't sleep, keep the fires burning for your comfort, and to heat up the coffee in case some concerned friends of Marco might drop by with news of him. Don't forget to lock the door bolts and be wary of strangers knocking at the door. We can't be too careful when we're out here in the sticks, so don't open the door for anybody you don't know."

"Marco is camping out in the mountains with his friends. Take care of yourself, and don't worry too much, Mama. We'll be home before daybreak. By the way, I informed the municipal police in San Antonio that Marco was missing. I furnished them with all the facts I know about the case, and they'll start their investigation," Toby said. "I was promised updates on the developments as they become available."

Toby knew Marco's preferred trail routes. They retraced the path he usually took across the valley, and down to the steep canyon trail and through the cable bridge. They ascended the trail leading to the wild berry field, or "blueberry hill," as Olin liked to call it.

Toby knew that Marco took this route only when he went hiking, not camping, but it was a site that must not be left out in their search for his brother.

They yelled out Marco's name many times, hoping that anyone out there would hear them and respond. There was no answer.

The searchers found faint footprints in the moist soil but they were unrecognizable due to the recent rains. They could not determine with certainty that they were impressions from Marco's hiking shoes, or from other hikers who might have picked berries and other wild fruits.

They moved on to inspect the base of the cliff for signs of a new campsite or an extinguished campfire. They found nothing.

Toby and Olin chose to stay away from the weathered cliff. It was not the place to find campers or hikers at night. They did not see any more footprints or any litter in the area that would indicate the recent presence of campers or hikers.

The search went on until the break of dawn, but they failed to find any clue that could lead them to Marco. "It's been a long twenty-four hours, Papa. Let's go home and continue our search in the morning. We eliminated the possibility of finding Marco here, and that's what we accomplished tonight. I'll take you to the sites where Marco and I camped with our friends."

Like Marco, Toby was an experienced mountain person. He told his parents that there were two things that might have caused him to get stuck in the wilderness. He could have met some friends in the mountains and camped with them, or, he may have encountered a setback that prevented him from coming home. "Marco and Aladdin may have been separated from Gizmo while they were on the trail. During a heavy tropical downpour or when thick fog blankets the area, it's not uncommon for people, or animals for that matter, to become confounded in such an environment. A spirited dog like Gizmo, who often leads the way and seldom follows, could have easily misplaced his direction. When he realized that the dog was missing, he would desperately try to search for him, or remain and wait there until they were reunited.

"If I were in Marco's shoes and got separated from Gizmo in the mountains, I wouldn't have the heart to leave the dog there alone. That could well be the reason for him remaining there.

"I can assure you both that Marco's fine. He's a mountaineer, and he knows these parts of the Caraballo Mountains very well. I simply refuse to accept that something serious has happened to him," Toby said.

Olin and Toby were exhausted and went to sleep. Amanda couldn't sleep a wink. She was bothered by the loud snores of the men, and very much worried about her missing son. She took out her rosary and prayed. "Dear God, please take care of Marco. Provide him a safe and swift passage from the mountains to our home, Amen."

Amanda's approaching birthday stirred up musings of the past. While she sat on her chair by the fire, she recalled that every year she marked that special day, she and Olin would look back at their first meeting with warm retrospection. How could she forget that day when she also celebrated her seventeenth birthday that same evening with her friends and classmates from the Saint Benedict Catholic High School?

"Those birthdays certainly evoke memories of our meeting many years ago," Olin said before her most recent birth anniversary.

"I can't believe it's been that long. We met twenty-three years ago but it seems like it was only yesterday," she recalled.

Olin met Amanda for the first time at the town market, and it wasn't their last meeting. Olin made sure of that. He continued to buy vegetables there on the Sundays he was off work, and walked her home after she closed her stall.

Leaning toward intellectual pursuits and driven toward success in her school activities, Amanda was the class valedictorian in all but her senior year in high school. She had become the editor of her school newsletter since her sophomore year. In her senior year, she was elected by the student body to be the president of the student council.

In contrast, Olin led a blue-collar lifestyle. His thick and callous hands were cut and scraped by underground rocks. He toiled long and hard in the mine, aiming for the coveted promotion as shift supervisor. Five years her senior, Olin was very enamored by Amanda's endearing traits and beauty.

Transcending dissimilar social and intellectual backgrounds, the pair took their friendship to a higher level in the weeks that followed.

One rainy morning, while they were talking about Amanda's forthcoming graduation, Olin summoned his mettle and popped the question: "Will you marry me, Amanda?"

She turned red and covered her face with her cupped hands. The timing of his proposal took her by surprise.

His voice still in a tremor, he went on to finish what he had started. "You know that I love you truly, and I would do anything to make you happy. I would cherish the opportunity to spend the rest of my life with you."

When she regained her composure, she said, "I understand how you feel about me, Olin, but I must graduate from high school first before making a jump like that. I admit that I expected you to ask me that question someday; but not today. And I can't defy my parents' wishes to pursue my college education."

"After those issues have been resolved, what would your answer to my question be?" he asked.

"In that case, my answer to your question would be an emphatic yes. There's no reason for you to doubt my words today, tomorrow, or ever, because you are the only man I really care for. I'm so much in love with you, Olin, and it's quite manifested by my actions when I'm by your side. Do you understand?" she said tearfully. She came short of asking him to remain safe and vigilant at work and not be distracted by talk of her "suitors" at school. The stories simply weren't true. After her confession, she would realize that those unsaid words of caution were no longer of consequence.

"One sticking point remains, however. College education requires years to carry through. Would you be willing to wait that long before we marry?" she asked.

"Listen carefully, my dear Amanda, as I have another proposal to make. It could hasten our wedding day without deviating from your personal goals."

Two weeks prior to Amanda's last day in high school and expecting that the couple would soon commence preparations to walk down the aisle together, family and friends were shocked to learn that Olin and Amanda had left town for the

Bicol Peninsula, which is located near the pacific shores on the southern tip of the island of Luzon. They had eloped to Olin's birthplace.

Amanda's parents, Gil and Marcia, were devastated by the news. They felt betrayed by their only child. "Was she coerced by Olin to run away from her family and everything she worked for in school?" her father asked.

"I'm not sure about your allegation, but I feel that Amanda was not pleased with the way we handled her affairs with Olin," her mother said.

"She's only seventeen, for heaven's sake! Shouldn't we get involved? We just can't leave her alone to face such a serious, life-changing issue."

"She's an intelligent person. With all the accolades and recognition, she has received in school so far, I believe she's capable and entitled to make her own choices," she said.

Meanwhile, more than a thousand kilometers away on the southern tip of the island, Olin's relatives arranged and scheduled all the events for the forthcoming wedding in the south.

Amanda and Olin were married by a Catholic priest on a lovely beach facing the warm Pacific Ocean. The ceremony was followed by a non-traditional early dinner made up mostly of seafood.

Tables were set and shielded from the tropical sun by palm leaves fastened to the top of the bamboo frames that were supported by posts dug into the sand. Boiled crabs, oysters, shrimp, large broiled tuna, and calamari were served with rice and chili-spiced taro leaves mixed with coconut milk. It was all carefully placed on top of the banana leaves that lined the tables. Amanda and Olin led the guests to the dinner tables.

The couple were serenaded with live music performed by a seven-instrument band. It was an impressive celebration, not seen in that town since the marriage of a congressman's brother.

That evening, following the beach ceremony and festivities, a public dance was held at the town plaza to honor the newlyweds. An integral part of the dance during wedding celebrations was the so called "money dance." It was intended for friends, family, and local politicians to contribute "start-up" funds for the new couple. While it generated a rousing fanfare, the usual amount of money raised was not much. For that reason, the rite was more symbolic than beneficial. Traditionally, the bride and the groom would dance with other partners while small amounts of money were pinned to their clothes. The money dance usually lasted from thirty minutes to an hour before the party revelers reverted to a traditional dance.

The next morning, Olin and Amanda spent their time on the beach, swimming, running, walking, sitting cozily, or laying on the pale brown sands. They watched the fishermen and the beachcombers go by.

"I've never been happier in all my life," she softly whispered in his ear. "So am I, Amanda. So am I. You are so young and so lovely, and I truly adore you."

Amanda worked full-time pursuing her college education. In less than four years, she finished her bachelor's degree in education, with honors, and became a high school teacher. She had followed in her father's footsteps.

She started her career as a substitute teacher in a public high school, and in just over a year, she became permanent as she replaced one of her retired colleagues.

They invited their close friends from the mine to a modest celebration of her success in her chosen profession. Everyone toasted the couple and wished them well when Amanda made a sudden announcement that she and Olin were expecting their first child. "Depending on the child's gender, the baby will be named Marco or Isabella," she said.

"My happiness would have been complete if my parents were here with us," Amanda said to Olin after their guests left. "After all, it was their hopes and dreams, not mine, that pushed me through college. And no disrespect was meant to you, Olin. You've helped me, inspired me, and given me every reason to attain that dream, even when dark clouds seemed to hover over our paths at times. Thank you so much, my love."

"You deserve all the success in the world, Amanda. You truly persevered, traveling constantly, and living in a cramped dormitory for many years, just so you could get through college."

As the season changed from dry to wet, and then to extremely wet, traveling between her school and her home became a strain on her. When the weather was inclement and transportation became such a problem, she often had to spend the night at a relative's house.

Amanda took her maternity leave of absence and extended

it a few times. She went back to work, but ended her teaching career when her other son, Toby, was born two years later. Raising her sons was the sole reason she did not find her way back to the teaching profession. Her father would comment, against her mother's dissension, that she relegated her career to being just a plain farm housewife.

Before the birth of Marco, she sent her parents several reconciliatory letters, but they were never opened. Fighting back tears, Amanda would ask Olin, "Did my parents completely close their doors to us? It's been five years since we last saw them. I've attempted to reconnect with them a few times to no avail. Why can't they forgive us?"

"Be patient, Amanda. I have a hunch that we will be reunited as a family again. It's about time," Olin said, gently caressing Amanda's baby bulge. "They will come to see us."

He was right. When Marco was born, Gil heard about it and decided it was time to be reconciled with Amanda and her family.

"Let's visit Amanda and Olin, not to mention the new member of the family I would love to meet. Enough is enough. I can no longer continue to live under false pretenses that everything's fine with our lives. We must see them this weekend."

The couple traveled to the mine to visit their only child and her husband, whom they had not seen in more than five years —and their little grandson.

"During the time we were separated from them, Amanda tried to get in touch with us but you slammed the door in her face. You never wanted me to open her letters," Marcia said. She was dying to see Amanda all those years, but Gil was too overbearing and refused to budge.

"Let bygones be bygones. A great refrain from a song of my time would say it all," Gil said. "A personal tenet taken too far can sever family ties. I suppose it's akin to a beast that needs to be shackled. If not, it could destroy us, and the people who matter most to us."

"Mama and Papa, pardon my interrupting your conversation, but I overheard the weighty issues that you were talking about. Olin and I presumed that you came to visit us with forgiving hearts, and I'm so glad we're right. I've sent you letters in the past asking for forgiveness and reconciliation. To this day, those letters still hold true for all intents and purposes, but you need not open them. We're family again, and that's all that matters now. I'm so overwhelmed with joy," she said, hugging her parents.

Lost in her recollections of her strained past, Amanda rose from her chair when she heard Olin stirring up from bed. She had cooked food for the men when she couldn't sleep that night. All she needed to do now was to heat it up when they were ready.

After several hours of sleep, Olin and Toby woke up smelling the aroma of the newly brewed Arabica coffee. For breakfast they had buttered sweet corn and sweet potatoes, paired with fried eggs and corned beef.

Rosie was back to work on the vegetable farm without Amanda for the first time. She hired temporary workers to catch up with the accrued work backlog, and to harvest some of the farm products. With or without Amanda, she would harvest and market the vegetables within the next few days.

Olin and Toby were getting ready to continue their search for Marco when a handful of students from the Saint Benedict Catholic High School arrived at the Vega farm to ask about

Marco, and to inform his family that they would help in the ongoing search. The students knew him in high school when he was a senior and they were in their freshman or sophomore years.

Jason Santos, the organizer of the group and a senior student, told the Vegas that there were only a few students available for the search, as the school was on a two-month summer break. Most students, he believed, were away, and did not hear about Marco's disappearance.

Amanda and Olin thanked the high school students and told them not to worry about their number. More searchers would join them when the news spread about Marco being missing. Olin told the group that the family appreciated all the help they could get from friends and local civic organizations.

"Your cousin, Jonah, will join our search group today and will meet us at the designated meeting place," Jason told Toby.

"Great," he replied. "More searchers mean we have a better chance of finding my brother. You can count on Jonah for assistance because he knows these mountains very well."

Toby told Jason and his group that his family considered Marco's disappearance a mystery, and still didn't have any knowledge of his whereabouts. He offered a suggestion that they might start their search around the area northwest of the canyon, particularly along the forested ridges. "The vast expanse along those ridges and slopes remain unsearched, and I'd always suspected that they were interesting areas to inspect. My father and I will continue our search in the north."

He described Marco's hiking shoes he wore the day he left, and the pattern that would be in any footprints left intact. This would be an identifier if they were lucky enough to find any. "It's almost certain that the heavy rains have washed all footprints, including those of our bay horse, Aladdin, and our black and brown German shepherd dog, Gizmo. We found faint footprints last night, but there was no way to determine if they were prints from Marco's shoes."

To conclude the pre-search meeting, Toby let the party know that the horse's mane and tail were sheared by Marco just before he rode out. This information could help in identifying the gelding.

Several concerned neighbors and friends visited Amanda to ask about Marco. Among them were two mothers of Toby's classmates who were with the student search group headed by Jason. She told them that her son had been missing for more than twelve days, and the search was on its third day. "The police are conducting their own search and investigation, as are certain individuals and local civic groups."

"Missing Person" signage with Marco's name and picture on them were posted on electric posts and concrete walls around the town and farm suburbs, she said.

Hoping for the best, she believed that her son and his friends were camping somewhere in the mountains. Quite possibly, he didn't have the chance to tell her that he would be away for an extended period of time.

Amanda invited the group to join her for a cup of coffee or tea, and some boiled sweet potatoes and sweet corn.

Olin and Toby were on their way to the two sites where Toby, Marco, and their friends had camped on many occasions.

They walked through the big valley and headed north, crossing a creek and irrigation conveyances that provided water for the farms. They hiked along the foothills while looking for footprints, or food and snack wrappings, or other litter. They found nothing.

They began their ascent. It was a tough uphill climb, causing them to stop and rest a few times along the way.

"Are we getting close to the top?" Olin asked.

"We should reach it in about a half-hour," Toby replied.

Stomping their feet on the plateau at last, Toby said, "This is the place we call Campground One. Check the views around you, Papa, while I search the site for campers."

Olin noticed that the clearing had almost a 360-degree view of the surrounding areas, including part of the big valley, the irrigation creek that runs through it, dwellings, and numerous patches of vegetable farms. He was clearly impressed with the different sceneries that could be viewed from all corners of the campground.

He walked across the level clearing and descended the short trail on the opposite end. There, he came across a group of women doing their washing chores near a spring water source. Parched campers and hikers benefited from the cool and refreshing water flowing out of the galvanized pipe. So did the women when they bathed and washed clothes.

"This is nature at its best, Toby, and I can now understand why you come here for camping," Olin said, as he retreated from the site. "I've just encountered a small group of topless females who were washing clothes next to the gushing spring water. I've heard about them before, but I hadn't seen them in the flesh until today."

In spite of his father's use of subtle words to describe the scene he just saw, Toby understood what he was trying to tell him. He and the other hikers and campers who frequented the camping areas were quite familiar with the way things are at the water source below.

He enlightened Olin that the women go naked from the

waist up only when they bathe and wash clothes there. "Papa, we shouldn't get too caught up with this issue, because the women bare their tops only for convenience, and without any intent of malice whatsoever. You have to believe and trust me on this matter. They do their washing chores here for lack of indoor plumbing in their homes."

Pointing at the lightly used road below, Toby said, "The women, who were raised in these nearby villages, hike that road to access the water source from their homes a few kilometers away. They treat this public amenity as their own laundry and wash rooms. They are entitled to share the water with everyone else, fully clothed or not."

Toby was told by a resident of a nearby village that the road below the water source was constructed by the now defunct Lagrimas Gold Mining Company, Inc., back in the late fifties. It had long been transferred to the provincial government and with it, the responsibilities for its maintenance.

"The provincial road is connected to the original mine road that leads to the old mill and mine site. Not many vehicles use this road, which is probably the reason proper maintenance is lacking. Not long ago, we passed through the gold mill via the mine and provincial roads on our way to Campground One," Toby said.

"Can we reach Campground Two by way of this road?"

"I'm afraid not. Going north will lead us to the relics of the old Lagrimas Gold Mine. The opposite way will take us to the town of Kamilagan. I don't see the need to go to either place at this time."

"Where could Marco and the other campers be?" Olin, who continued walking without expecting an immediate answer from Toby, asked. Since the time they began their search for Marco, they had not encountered one group of hikers or campers in the mountains.

Toby led his father to the other site where they had frequently camped before. They descended the trail from the plateau and traveled westward.

Along the trail, they stopped to watch a group of monitor lizards, averaging two meters in length, who had converged on a rocky area to sun themselves.

Toby tutored Olin on reptiles, explaining that lizards were often seen sunning themselves in clearings, on rocky areas, and even roads that were lightly used. "When they see vehicles passing through, they quickly scamper out of the way. Reptiles are cold-bloodied animals that need outside heat to help them digest their food. Most of their body systems, including digestion, are highly dependent on the temperature."

The lizards disappeared quickly when they saw Olin and Toby approaching them to take a closer look. "They move incredibly fast for their size," Olin said.

Olin and Toby followed the beaten trail while crossing cable-plank bridges, spanning two ravines, and passing through farms and meadows until they reached the Santa Ana Rainforest.

The duo sat to rest and eat their sandwiches. It was a perfect time to sip strong, black coffee from their thermos bottles.

The early afternoon sun was now blocked by rain clouds and a stiff breeze began to blow northwesterly. Without warning, rain started to drop in torrents.

Olin and Toby quickly dashed beneath the rainforest's thick canopy to stay out of the rain.

They took their raincoats from their knapsacks and slipped them on to provide additional protection from the rain and possible attacks of leeches. These tormenting parasite found in dense tropical jungles could attach themselves to the skin and gain nourishment by feasting on blood.

"Leeches are almost as bad as disease-causing mosquitoes, or poisonous plants that will make you itch for weeks after contact," Toby said.

Olin noticed the presence of coffee plants at the outskirts of the rainforest. Half of the beans were deep red and ready for picking. Toby explained that the coffee plants are grown and harvested by the people farming in the area.

"Certain varieties of coffee thrive well in the rainforest's high moisture and warm climate, but like other fruit or seed-bearing plants they need the sun, and that's the reason they don't grow well inside the thickly forested areas."

While they waited for the rain to stop, Olin and Toby walked through the flora under the dense canopy, observing the diverse wildlife and the natural beauty of the tropical rainforest. They noted that it was vegetated with thousands of plants of different varieties, from the ground to the top. The trees were growing old; their trunks and branches covered with thick mosses. Green ferns, pitcher plants, and exotic orchids had abundant growth. The orchids and other flowering plants seemed to attract bees and butterflies, and many other pollinating agents.

Olin and Toby continued their search for Marco as soon as the heavy rain turned to light drizzle. "We are about half an hour away from Campground Two," Toby said.

After leaving the rainforest area, Olin and Toby ascended a trail that took them to the old logging road that had been abandoned for decades. They walked on what was left of the road for more than three kilometers. They crossed fallen trees, road cuts, and landslides, until they were on the ridge overlooking a small creek.

Toby led his father down to the grassy area next to the creek. "This is Campground Two," he said.

"It's an ideal site for camping, near the creek, and so scenic and quiet; but it doesn't look like anybody has visited the place for months," Olin said.

Toby concurred. He was now beginning to wonder where Marco and his friends were. He had hoped and expected that campground two was where they would find his brother and his friends camping.

"I've shown you our two favorite campsites, Papa. Campgrounds One and Two look as if they've been unvisited for some time. Maybe...if spring water were flowing through a pipe somewhere near the creek area, this place would be teeming with topless women."

Olin, in his calm way, scoffed at Toby's prank. He wasn't impressed at all. "This isn't the right time to be dishing out jokes. Not until we learn that Marco is safe, wherever he is."

He asked if there were other campgrounds they had not checked.

"This is the second of the two campgrounds where we usually pitch our tents. We checked both and found them to appear unoccupied, for weeks or even months. Would Marco or his companions know of other camping places I've never heard of?"

The father and son team plodded through another disappointing day in the mountains. They made detours many times to visit places that even Toby was unfamiliar with. They had hoped to find a clue that might lead to the unraveling of the Marco Vega mystery.

Still not having a single clue to his whereabouts, those

involved with the search were wary that they didn't have a thing to identify with nor focus on. There was really nothing on which to hang their hopes. They could rightly associate the term "mystery" to Marco's disappearance. Yearning for a clue, Toby and Olin believed something positive would turn up sometime soon.

The men agreed that it was time to go home, rest, and prepare to resume their search in the morning.

"Amanda must be so worried about Marco. We must go, Toby. I'm very much concerned for your mother. She's alone, and she's been through a lot of late. Let's hope that Marco is safe and well, and surviving on jungle resources as I would think he is."

Toby figured that it was faster to reach home by going back to the old logging road and then down the trail toward the rainforest. Before they reached the fringes of the rainforest, they would then take the backdoor; the southwest trail that would lead them back to the big valley and home.

The Caraballo Mountains, visible from the southwest trail, would guide them if they lost the old trail.

Just then, the duo spotted a noisy bunch of brown monkeys playing in a tree. The apes produced loud, screeching sounds as they jumped from one branch to the next. They were quite rambunctious, to describe them mildly. The men heard the ruckus and walked closer to the tree to watch the monkeys romp on the tree branches. They were so amused watching the apes play that they decided to stay a few minutes longer.

All of a sudden, they heard high-pitched whistles from the sky.

"What are those sounds, and where are they coming from?" Olin asked.

"I don't know. It's probably a hawk or another bird of prey

looking for food."

Almost at the same time, they looked skyward and discovered a huge bird circling with its broad wings extended.

"It's much too huge to be a hawk. It must be an eagle," Toby said. "A giant eagle?"

More than a mile away, across the cloudless sky, the eagle spotted its prey hanging from the branch of a tree. Not wasting time, it dove from the sky with such amazing swiftness that the unsuspecting monkeys were caught unaware. It rolled ninety degrees to its left and grabbed the monkey that was hanging from the lowest branch. With its prey tucked in its powerful talons, the eagle flew north.

"That was indeed an amazing display of speed and agility. The huge eagle almost matched the quickness and grace of a much smaller hawk," Toby said.

Olin was likewise fascinated. "I'm sure your mother would be thrilled to listen to my story about the eagle."

"And don't forget Marco, too, when he comes home. He'll be a biologist one day, and I'll bet he would love to hear our story about the predator," Toby said, shaking his head in awe after watching the eagle's sleek maneuver. It was the first time either one had seen an eagle fly, and to observe such impressive hunting prowess.

"I was not aware of such a presence in these mountains," Olin said.

Checking his watch, Toby noted that he and his father had spent more than ten hours in their search. It was time to go home.

Upon their arrival at the farm, Olin and Toby learned from Amanda that the municipal police had questioned five of

Marco's friends whom Toby believed had gone camping with him. Three of them; David, Ramon, and Pablo, told the police that they had not left town recently. Witnesses saw them play basketball at the town plaza almost every day. The other two, Hector and Carlito, went to Baguio right after the start of the summer break to attend the wedding of a friend.

None of Marco's close friends had seen him lately, let alone gone camping in the mountains with him. They were shocked to learn that he was missing. Those physically able would join the search party when it is reconvened the next morning.

The police report didn't bode well for Olin and Amanda. They couldn't believe that Marco would camp alone in the wilderness for more than just a few days. "Something's wrong," Olin said. Toby, undeterred as ever, thought otherwise. "Something's keeping him there. We'll find out soon."

CHAPTER 12
THE SEARCH CONTINUES

Jason noticed hoofprints on the ground, almost washed out by the rains, but still showing distinct horseshoe impressions. "Look at those marks on the ground. Do they resemble hoofprints?" he asked his companions.

The male eagle landed on the cliff ledge with his prey, a wild rabbit. Craving food and getting weaker every minute, Marco was pleased to see the rabbit dropped on the ledge. "I must partake in this feast. I hope they'll share some of the meat with me."

The male eagle was not on friendly terms with Marco, but the predator settled down as soon as he heard the shrill whistles coming from the six-hole bamboo flute.

"What a contrast with yesterday's acrimonious meeting," he observed. "The wind gadget works just as the wildlife photographer told Mama. It's quite amazing."

Holding the flute, Marco reached and touched the lion-like mane of the male eagle. It allowed him to do so while the female eagle watched. As he was stroking the eagle's plumage, he noticed that some of the primary feathers on his right wing were either ruffled, damaged, or missing. "This eagle seems to be growing imperfect feathers to replace the few that are missing. Or maybe not at all. It's hard to tell while crouching on this cramped space," he observed. While his aim was to tame and make friends with the wild predators, it wasn't his job, nor would he attempt to try and find the reason why there was a minor impairment on his wing. "I see no need to find details of the injury or what had caused it—the eagle is stellar in his aerial maneuvers, and his great hunting skills are rivaled only by his mate."

He continued to smooth the eagle's feathers, his hands converging on the ruffled feathers of his right wing. He shifted his gaze to the giant eagle's long, yellow legs and his sharp, dark claws.

To his surprise, the eagle slowly spread his wings and walked a full step toward him. Marco took it as his acceptance to the flock. He was now on friendly terms with both winged hunters.

He had his mother and Mr. Madera to thank, for without the bamboo flute, or wind gadget as he called it, he'd still be trying to find ways to tame the wild predators.

His relationship with the eagles began on a high note. He had hoped that it would be a great friendship that would continue long after he was back at home. "A friendship beyond the ledge would be great, especially when I become a full-fledged biologist and have a role in the eagles' captive breeding program."

The newly forged friendship would be tested in a moment. He would find out if the eagles were willing to give him a share of the rabbit meat. He would need to make a quick move, because the eagles were hungry and about to tear the rabbit apart on their own.

Marco held the rabbit in his hand while watching the reactions of both eagles. They seemed defiant in the beginning but later allowed him to hold and lay the prey down on the ledge. With his sharp Swiss army knife, he sliced the rabbit and gave chunks of the meat to each eagle. He kept a choice of part of the rabbit for himself and continued to slice the rest of the meat into smaller parts and gave the pieces to each of them until they were full.

When the eagles were resting inside their nest, Marco sliced the rabbit meat he had set aside for himself. He removed the skin and gave it back to the eagles to scavenge. The remaining meat portion was lean, and suitable for sun drying.

With the use of twigs from the nest, he fashioned a simple frame to aid the drying of the sliced meat. Barring an overcast sky, he estimated that it would take at least a day and a half to two days of exposure to the sun before he could attempt to eat any of it.

Marco was right in guessing that the male eagle would be out to hunt again. The high-flying eagle dove from the ledge and glided almost without effort as he flew south toward the big valley. Headed to their customary hunting range, the eagle chose not to perform his spectacular flying display this time.

Marco had read from one of his books that the male and female eagle partners either hunt together or separately. He would certainly love to see the predators fly off the ledge and hunt together. *"That would be a near-perfect day for the pair I haven't seen hunt together. In their search of prey, they seem independent of each other."*

His rancorous association with the eagles behind him, he maintained a close bond with them—a big step in the right direction, since it meant boosting his chances of survival on the ledge.

Jason and his search party planned to hike northwest

of the canyon as Toby had suggested. New additions to the party necessitated dividing into sub-groups. This would avoid crowding on the narrow paths and would speed up the search.

He asked members of the party to fan out in order to cover a wider area and assigned two of the most experienced trail hikers as leaders of the other two sub-groups.

One of the leaders, Toby's friend Reggie, requested those who were wearing timepieces to synchronize their watches.

"That's a good idea," Jason said. "At the end of the day, between five and five thirty in the afternoon, we'll meet here for the end-of-day roll call. Then we'll hike home together. We will still follow the same routine, but with our watches synchronized, we can improve our time management."

Jonah, Henry, and Jason separated from the other members of the party and embarked north instead of northwest. Young and able bodied, the three high school seniors covered much ground, as they had in past days.

They blazed a new trail when they couldn't find a trace of the old one. The trio walked into the old trail at some point and were pleasantly surprised.

Jonah, who did not wear prescription glasses, was given the responsibility to use the binoculars to check out the ridges and valleys for signs of an existing or former campground. "If a bay horse and a black and brown German shepherd dog show up on your scope, they can lead us to Marco," Jason said.

Occasionally, when Jonah had to rest his eyes, he handed the binoculars to Henry.

The youngsters wanted to complete most of their search before the afternoon downpour, because the rain would reduce their visibility, and the ground would become muddy in many areas.

After a brief rest following their lunch, they resumed their uphill hike. They reached the ridge for the first time in their search.

Jason noticed hoofprints on the ground, almost washed out by the rain, but still showing distinct horseshoe impressions. "Look at those marks on the ground. Do they resemble hoofprints?" he asked his companions.

"Those marks were definitely made by a horse," Jonah said. "If there are hoofprints around, there must be a horse grazing nearby."

When he focused his binoculars on the distant hillsides, Jonah saw something move. He cleaned and readjusted his lenses. Training his scope on the same spot, he saw a horse's tail swing around to slap away flies from its hind legs.

Jonah handed the binoculars to Jason and said, "Look at the slopes to your left just below the clump of acacia trees. There's a horse grazing there."

Wiping his sweaty pair of prescription glasses, Jason said, "Where's the clump of acacia trees you mentioned? Ah, there it is." He peered through his binoculars and bellowed, "That indeed is a horse! By the way, it's brown. What's the color of Marco's horse?"

"Bay or reddish brown."

To avoid frightening the horse and create unnecessary problems, Jonah suggested to his friends that he alone must approach and take control of the horse.

"Go get him, Jon. You're just as experienced with horses as your cousin Marco. You're in his league when it comes to roping and riding horses," Jason said, turning around to give Henry a wink and a smile.

Jonah offered the bay horse a piece of dried fruit he was saving for his snack. The steed took the bait while the boy grabbed the stray rope attached to the hackamore. He now had full control of the horse.

"There's no doubt in my mind that this is Marco's horse. I've heard a lot of good things about this gelding, although I never had the chance to pat, stroke, or take him for a ride," he said.

With raised eyebrows, he noticed how every riding paraphernalia was neatly strapped to the horse. It was no surprise to him at all because he'd known Marco long enough to observe how he liked to organize things thoroughly, including the way he prepared a horse before he took him for a quick sprint.

Jason and Henry were likewise amazed at how detailed and well-ordered Marco had packed his camping gear and supplies. They found the utility and supply bags secured in the back of the saddle, and the camping gear fastened to the front. The stirrups were hanging high and tied to each side of the saddle, and the bridle and other miscellaneous items were kept inside the utility bag. Canned and dried food, rice, brown sugar, dog food, and a small and unused rice pot were stashed inside the supply bag.

"Since we found his horse still saddled and free to move about, where do you think Marco is?" Henry said.

"We're here to find out. We can only hope that he's safe somewhere and is aware that help is on the way," Jason said.

"Marco must have sheared his mane and tail in a hurry," Jonah said while he was unsaddling the horse to dry the saddle pads and other leather accessories. He took some of the brown sugar from the supply bag and offered it to the gelding, who licked it clean off his palm.

Once Jonah tied the horse to a tree, the party commenced looking around for human footprints, or any evidence that people had camped in the area at one time or another. Having located Marco's horse, the boys found more strength in their search for him. They combed a wide area for hours before they were convinced that no one but the horse had set foot in the vicinity for some time.

The boys ended their day in the mountains and went back to their designated meeting place.

While Jason and Jonah took the horse back to the Vega farm in the valley, Henry waited for the other members of the search party to arrive. Once all were accounted for, they started heading for home.

Marco was snoozing when one of the eagles dropped a monkey on the cliff ledge. He woke up yawning and quickly cut the prey with his sharp knife. He handed over pieces to the hungry eagles, keeping a choice cut for himself.

He eyed the improvised sun-drying rack to make sure he had enough meat in the cycle to last him until the eagles' next hunt, taking into consideration the number of days required for drying. Inspecting a slice of the rabbit meat that hung from the drying rack, it appeared to need more time in the sun. He was getting weaker while he waited for the meat to dry sufficiently. He cut the big slice into smaller chunks and began to chew one for the first time. He thought the taste was funny, and would need to develop an acquired taste for it. Eating uncooked, sun-dried meat was inconceivable to him. This time, he had no other choice. He needed quick nourishment.

The young man recalled his childhood days when his mother stayed by his side at the table and reminded him to take his time eating and to chew his food thoroughly.

Well, he did exactly that when he began eating the sundried rabbit meat. He would have to survive on a solely protein diet.

To consume the meat with more bravado was what he could hope for.

"The female eagle is out on a hunt. I've been wanting meat that gives me no problems when I eat it. I'm hoping the predator will find a good prey."

Marco reorganized his small space on the ledge. Using a few more loose rocks lying on the platform, more twigs from the nest, and his plastic raincoat, he improvised to make his water collecting system semi-permanent. Frequent rains provided him with enough supply of drinking water and some extra to wash his face and body.

When the raincoat was not in use collecting rainwater, it blocked most of the sun's rays during the day and gave him some protection from the breeze at night.

"So far, so good. The meat has to be dried longer and it will, once I have more raw meat in the cycle. It's a temporary setback that will get better in time. My water supply is more than sufficient for my needs, thanks to my improved water recovery system."

Art Holly was unsettled with the news that his mine foreman, Olin Vega, had a son that had been missing. After hearing the details of the ongoing search, he determined that an aerial search might help. He phoned Robert Gunn, an acquaintance and a member of the board of directors of Northern Consolidated Copper Mine, to inquire about the feasibility of utilizing one of Robert's planes "to search for possible clues that might help the searchers on the ground locate Marco Vega, who had mysteriously disappeared after taking the trail in the wilderness with his horse and dog."

Marc Valdez, a former Philippine Airlines captain and currently a senior pilot with Gunn Charter Flights, received an urgent call from Robert Gunn, the owner of the company. Captain Valdez, as he is known in the office, was instructed by his boss to fly a Cessna 310 aircraft to Bagarran Municipal Airport in Nueva Vizcaya and await further directives there. He was briefed by Robert on his search mission, and was asked if he was ready to switch hats for a different undertaking. He offered quick assurances that the project was not poles apart from the aerial photography assignments he had carried out every so often. He would have supported the use of a rotary-wing aircraft for the job if it was proposed, or if his opinion was sought.

Because of the fact that Toby was familiar with the trails and possible detours that Marco might have taken, he was chosen to guide the flight crew.

That morning, instructions were wired to Toby to take the bus bound for Northern Consolidated Copper Mine. He was informed that his task would be to help the flight crew find signs that would indicate the presence of Marco in the area, and with some luck, may lead the ground searchers to his location.

Gunn Charter Flights made arrangements with a local fuel trader to provide aviation fuel at the Bagarran Municipal Airport.

A Toyota Land Cruiser from the mine transported Toby to the airport. Maps of the area and written instructions for the aerial search were provided to the pilot.

Toby promptly marked the suggested flight path and the hot areas on the map while the plane was being refueled by the two-man flight crew.

Captain Valdez raced down the runway and gently manipulated the flight controls of the twin engine Cessna aircraft to a smooth liftoff. He and Tony Aguilar, the co-pilot, maintained a safe altitude, as they were aware of the high peaks they would have to circumvent or fly over.

Toby felt a lump in his throat when he recognized the terrain he had traveled on foot with Marco and some of their friends in the past. He missed his brother.

If Marco had gotten bogged down in the mountains, Toby hoped the aerial surveillance would help uncover a trace of his location.

The air searchers winged toward the northeast past Campground One, and then flew north to survey Campground Two. They stayed on their planned course and inspected the old mine and mill site.

Farther north, Toby spotted a huge eagle soaring parallel to their flight path but on a much lower altitude. In as much as the plane and the eagle were on the same course, he determined the eagle's flight direction simply by asking Captain Valdez what his flight heading was. When he checked back on the eagle, he noticed that the predator had completely disappeared from his sight. He knew that it must have landed somewhere but he failed to determine where its flight had terminated. "No big deal." He felt it was nothing to be excited about because he and his father had recently watched a similar eagle hunting in a nearby forest. Nevertheless, he called the air crew's attention to inform them that the eagles were known to live and hunt only in the distant rainforest of the Sierra Madre Mountains. "I've been surprised to see eagles in these mountains in recent weeks," he said.

"I never would have known that the eagles are found only in the Sierra Madre Mountains if you hadn't told me, Toby. Tony, did you know that for a fact?"

"No, Captain, I wasn't aware of that," he said. "I know of their existence on the islands, but I don't know exactly where they live and hunt for food."

They were in the air for over an hour, and, except for the sighting of the eagle, their mission had been uneventful.

"Captain," Toby said, "I pointed out to you all the suspected spots and the routes and detours I thought my brother would have taken. I'm quite disappointed that we didn't see anything that would reveal his presence in the area. I was hoping that I would spot the dog, too. Now it's up to you to decide where to take the air search next."

"Son, it will be dark in a couple of hours, and we have about forty-five minutes of fuel left in the tank to get us back to the municipal airport. Let's call it a day and resume our search tomorrow."

Bright and early, Captain Valdez and company began their second day of air search. The flight crew maintained a course parallel to the south-flowing Adaro River.

Thanks to the heavy seasonal rains that usually came at this time of the year, the formidable Adaro was flowing through narrow waterways and over big, rounded boulders, creating a rapid and turbulent flow, and then gradually transforming into serene current downstream in the wider and less graded sections.

Toby recalled the fun that he, Marco, and their friends had when they leisurely walked and sunned themselves on the sandy riverbanks.

"To tread upon your earthy till, and frolic on your river sands," he recited Marco's often repeated lines from the verse "On Eagle's Wings."

The airborne searchers reached the confluence of the Adaro and Malaya rivers that converged to form the mighty

Calamatan River, whose powerful current appeared to have bisected mountains centuries ago and was now snaking across the flatlands on its way out to sea.

While crossing the Calamatan River in the air, Toby recalled the proposed construction of a hydro-electric dam that was envisaged by authorities but vehemently opposed by the people whose farms would be inundated if the project went through.

Captain Valdez made a sweeping turn to the right, heading northeast and upstream of the Malaya River.

Toby was in awe as he viewed the hundreds of rice paddies, cornfields, dwellings, and green vegetable patches on both sides of the river. He had seen them all while traveling on foot, but this was the first time he'd seen the passing scenery from an airplane.

The green and amber terraces of grain contrasted with the weathered gray background of meticulously interlocked stone walls that enclosed and held the rice paddies in place.

He saw cattle grazing on the gentler slopes. His jaw dropped when he spotted a lone white cow appearing like a ghost in the midst of a predominantly brown herd. "I've seen and heard of albino animals, but I have never seen an albino cow before."

For the young outdoorsman who grew up roving the rugged countryside—the copper and gold mining complex where he and Marco spent their early years, the terraced grain plantations, the green meadows, the undulating rivers and tributaries, the canyons and cliffs, the mountains and rainforests, and the vegetable and crop farms—the glimpses of the scenery from the plane were simply breathtaking.

On the final round of their reconnaissance flights over the stretch of land southwest of Mount Malvar, Captain Valdez took the aircraft as low as possible to provide them a closer look at the location where Aladdin was found. No one appeared to be in the area.

Assured that all the hot spots marked on the map were searched, and every dubious sight checked, the air crew resolved that continued investigation of the suspect sites by ground searchers was deemed necessary.

After two days of extensive aerial search, the plane crew decided to suspend the air operation until further advised.

Mike Ramirez, a reporter from the San Antonio Weekly Gazette, arrived at the Vega farm to interview Amanda and Olin in regard to the disappearance of Marco.

After Olin had answered all the questions Mike would ask, the reporter scribbled some notes and asked him if he wanted to make a statement to the press and what message, if any, he wanted to convey to the readers. Olin asked Amanda to provide the statement, and she complied.

"On behalf of my family—my husband, Olin, and my son, Toby—I would like to express our deepest gratitude for the overwhelming support we have received from Marco's friends and schoolmates at the Saint Benedict Catholic High School, the municipal police, civic groups, employees of the Northern Consolidated Copper Mines, our business associates, and our friends.

"Marco's been missing for more than twelve days now, and if anyone can provide a clue to his whereabouts, we would like to know. You can inform us directly, or through the San Antonio Weekly Gazette.

"These tension-filled days have been very difficult for our family and friends, but as we continue our search, we are optimistic that we will soon hear good news about him.

"We've received monetary contributions from various companies, civic groups, businesses, and private individuals. We will use the money to create more signage and expand our radio broadcasts to cover other areas as well.

"To our benefactors, friends, and supporters, we thank you all so much," she said.

Marco was standing on the ledge when the female eagle landed with her prey. He quickly strode over to gently pat and soothe the eagle's feathers in appreciation of her success in the hunt.

Not wasting more time than necessary, he proceeded to cut the monkey and save his portion of the meat for sun-drying.

The eagles had become more tolerant of Marco, particularly with the way he apportioned their food. He cut and rationed the meat chunks to each adult eagle the way he saw fit, giving a bit more to the hungrier and more aggressive one.

Except when they scavenged the carcasses of their prey, the eagles used their beaks sparingly with Marco on the ledge slicing the meat.

Marco chewed the dried meat thoroughly. He soon learned that the more he chewed the meat, the more palatable it would become.

When the eagles finished their food and had settled down, Marco resumed socializing with them. He was guided by the eagles' responses to his actions. He did many things that popped in his mind, such as stroking their manes and wings while talking or whispering to them.

The predators could not comprehend any of the words he spoke, although they seemed intent on watching him very closely. Their sharp eyes constantly followed his every movement, no matter how routine his actions were.

CHAPTER 13
ALARMING NEWS REPORT

*"This is very strange," he said. "Monkey-eating eagles
don't normally exist in those mountains. Two separate
witnessed reports of huge predators hunting in different
areas there, three days apart, sounds credible."*

Mayor Gene was having breakfast with his wife, Juanita, on a warm and sunny morning in their home in Santa Teresa.

He browsed the well-circulated San Antonio Weekly Gazette while sipping hot coffee. A news report caught his eye, an article entitled "Huge Eagles seen in San Antonio." Gene continued to read the news report alleging that farmers saw a huge eagle hunting for food near the big valley, a farm in the suburbs of San Antonio.

Three days later, the article went on, deer trappers reportedly saw at least two giant monkey-eating eagles hunting in the Caraballo Mountains not far from the Santa Ana Rainforest.

"This is very strange," he said. "Monkey-eating eagles don't normally exist in those mountains. Two separate witnessed reports of huge predators hunting in different areas there, three days apart, sounds credible."

When Gene finished his breakfast, he read the news report again and called it to the attention of his wife. "Juanita, read this front-page article and please give me your take on it."

After reading the article, she dropped the paper and said, "Gene, I didn't know eagles existed in that part of the islands."

"I know, and you're right on that assumption; but here's my point and let me explain. Do you remember what we experienced in this town more than two years ago?"

"Yes, I do remember those big, hungry eagles that had created some problems here."

"Now we are on the same page. Two years ago, we drove a pair of giant eagles and an eaglet away from the Santa Magdalena Rainforest because the adult predators attacked and carried off some of our farmers' livestock here in Santa Teresa. We succeeded in driving them away. Or so we thought," he said.

"What do you mean by that? Didn't you drive the eagles away for good?" she asked.

"This news report gives me the creeps. Something tells me that I should investigate this and find out if those eagles indeed reached the northeast Sierra Madre Mountains, or diverted their path to the Caraballo Mountains instead," he said.

"Are you telling me that the eagles relocated to the Caraballo Mountains instead of dispersing to the northeast?"

"I'm not saying they definitely did, but if that's what has happened, it may be worth looking into."

"How do you know that those were the same eagles you drove away? Should we be disturbed by the news without knowing where the predators came from? Are they bothering anyone in that community?"

"No, but if you remember, it was my plan to drive them far and out of range of our farmers' livestock, and to also keep them out of harm's way. Where they ended up could be anybody's guess, but I believe that the Caraballo Mountains is a strong possibility. I would feel responsible for those predators if they were to end up near the populated communities and started terrorizing the domestic farmers there. It may be time to visit San Antonio and find out if these are the same eagles that pestered our livestock farmers here more than two years ago. If so, I want to know if they are hunting wild animals, domestic livestock, or both, just as they did in our locale. I dread the thought that people would suffer because of our actions in the past. We could provide them advice based on what we've experienced here."

"Your concern sounds reasonable, but I think that you must wait a few more days for fresh news about the eagles, and to deliberate on what course of action to take before that long bus trip to San Antonio," she said.

"You're right. Let's wait for a few days then," he said.

As much as Gene was compelled to visit San Antonio at the earliest possible time, he needed a few extra days to see the progress of the final phase of his irrigation infrastructure project in San Angelo.

After graduating from the Green Valley Institute of Technology in Manila with a degree in civil engineering, Gene's son, Gener, took over the management of the San Salvador Construction Company that his father had founded. The elder Salvador had decided to enter local politics. Retained as a consultant to his company, Gene was endorsed as a candidate and was elected as the mayor of Santa Teresa, a position he currently held for a second term.

Gene started his construction company eighteen years ago with only a handful of employees. Currently, the company's variable labor force on its peak operation could go up to thirty men and women, of which more than three-quarters of the force were skilled workers: drivers, equipment operators, welders, repair and maintenance technicians, and drafters.

Barring unforeseen delays, which in most cases could be attributed to bad weather this time of the year, the project would be expected for completion in fifteen days.

Marco was half-awake on the ledge when the male eagle dropped a two-meter-long snake on the ledge next to the nest.

"It looks like a python to me. It has no fangs or poison sacs behind its jaws," he said, rubbing his sleepy eyes.

He quickly cut the lifeless reptile into chunks and routinely rationed it to the hungry eagles.

Marco quickly glanced at his drying rack to make sure that he had enough monkey and rabbit meat to last him for at least three more days. Unless he was too hungry and there wasn't enough to eat, he preferred to stay away from reptile meat. He dried his share of the snake and lizard meat, just like the rest of his share, but to be given away as training incentives. He might decide, from time to time, to give the eagles rewards when they obeyed his commands, or when they were back from a successful hunt.

He learned from his short association with the winged predators that their food type varied at times. He couldn't predict the kind of prey each eagle brought to the ledge. The kind of prey they hunt depends on the time of the hunt and the area where the predators forage.

"Several days ago, the eagles' prey was a one-meter-long

monitor lizard. Today, it's a python. What will it be next?"

Adapting well to his raw meat diet, Marco had somewhat blended in with the giant eagles in terms of the food they all consumed. He had lived with the predators for fifteen days. He counted three tallies he had scratched on the rock wall. "It's been that long since I got myself into this mess."

He felt he had lost some weight because of his poor and unbalanced diet. He had cravings for certain foods that he used to eat at home on a regular basis, but he was able to block them all from his mind.

Marco believed that his family and friends, searching for him with every resource they had, may not be able to find him as soon as they would like. The ledge would be difficult to spot from the ground because of the growth of vegetation above and below it.

His mobility on the ledge was constrained by limited space, thus preventing him from conducting a detailed investigation of both flanks of the cliff to try and find a safe escape without the help of rock climbing paraphernalia.

He had doubts that he could be spotted by searchers flying overhead in a fixed-wing aircraft.

Marco understood the basic necessities involved in the search for a missing person in the mountains. Knowledge of the area, the ability to organize, and the obvious logistics are but a few things to consider. As had always been the case, bad weather presented a big problem, and couldn't be taken for granted when scouring the wilderness at this time of the year. He was confident, however, that the men in the family, along with capable friends, could take on such tasks even during stormy days.

He had always kept his family in his thoughts. "They're all badly missed," he murmured. "Does anyone in the family believe that I am still alive? I sure hope so. I know that Toby is aware that if I get stuck in a bad place in the mountains, I can survive, nurse my lumps, and move on."

Marco did not think his mother would share Toby's conviction. While Amanda had told him on several occasions that he was far too mature for his age, he believed that she would not infer a close correlation between maturity and hardiness.

His father would likely agree with Toby. "Papa, a mining man all his life, has attributes that far outweigh his lack of experience in the mountains. For one thing, he is a glass-half-full person. He has survived accidents in the underground mine where he works, the latest in which he and his crew were trapped for more than five days. He believes that the accident could have been prevented if the surface water diversion system had been properly maintained. In other words, complacency largely contributed to the accident." In situations where hikers or campers get disoriented and are lost in the forest, he pointed out that they will seek refuge and find food from indigenous plants and animals to survive while waiting for their impending rescue.

Despite his current difficulties, Marco maintained a very close association with the eagles. He was always in high spirits when the flock was on the ledge with him—perhaps akin to the joy pet owners experience when their pets are with them.

When he was not tending to his meager needs, he was brainstorming; finding ways to get off of the ledge, and weighing his few options to determine the most viable choice of pursuit.

As he straddled the line between an early "escape" fraught with danger, and awaiting a safe rescue that might take longer and extend his stay on the eagles' ledge, the first option would likely be his choice.

Since an early rescue on the high ledge didn't seem forthcoming, Marco conjured a crafty but daring scheme to break out of the very unique and dangerous web he had inadvertently got caught in. His escape would require a thoroughly trained giant eagle to fly him down from the ledge. They would ride the thermals and updrafts generated by the high winds and rugged topography of the area. Then they would flap down toward the bottom of the cliff, a vertical separation of about seventy-five meters.

"There's no easy way out. Dire circumstances call for drastic measures. Unless a clever idea drops out of the sky and changes the whole situation, there is no perceivable means of escape other than what I have devised."

The escape plan, Marco's central focus, would work only if one of the eagles was trained sufficiently to do its part. It would entail intensive drills and coordination with the eagle he would choose to carry out the escape. From all indications, the female eagle had the edge over her mate by virtue of her size advantage. Once formulated, the plan must be tested repeatedly until Marco was convinced that it was reasonably safe enough to proceed with it. He had everything to lose if he were to fall off the cliff as a result of a faulty miscalculation or insufficient training of the eagle.

If he could minimize the perils involved in the getaway, he would carry it out at the earliest possible time. Spending more than two weeks on the eagles' ledge was about all he could take. He must find a way to free himself of his "captivity" as soon as he could reduce the risks involved.

Though he had seldom sidestepped risky activities, Marco acknowledged that he was not bound by hopelessness and would not act in a reckless manner. He knew that he would be rescued one day, but didn't know when that would happen.

He continued to train the eagles to respond when a command was given. He limited his commands to phrases he would expect to use during the getaway. He would, on occasion, use the four-finger, under-the-tongue whistle to spur the eagles to fly toward him.

Like clockwork, he gave away rewards in the form of small reptile meat chunks when he observed satisfactory responses to his commands.

Next, he named the female eagle Simidar, and the male predator Hannibal.

To begin the next lesson—name and voice recognition—Marco devised command phrases for Simidar and Hannibal. He shouted commands after their names were called and results began to show promise. After days of arduous training, the eagles exhibited acceptable improvements with their responses.

Encouraged by the results, Marco repeated the drill several times daily while Simidar or Hannibal were on the ledge with him. He spent more time training Simidar, but he trained Hannibal as well, when the female eagle was out on a hunt.

The drill was set in motion when Marco commanded Simidar to fly off the ledge, circle around once, and fly back to the ledge, landing on the knapsack.

He had cut a piece of cloth from his trousers and wrapped it around Simidar's leg for protection against injury from the string when it tightens.

He then tied one end of 2.5 mm cotton twine around the eagle's protected leg, and then goaded it to fly off the ledge. He allowed just the right amount of slack for the predator to fly straight out, circle around, and then fly back when she experienced the pullback of the string.

Marco added the final components of his planned course of action as the training progressed. After the eagle circled around and returned to the ledge, she was promptly tasked by Marco to grasp the rock-weighted knapsack, heave it, and fly off the ledge in one fluid motion. The giant eagle flew back to the ledge with the weighted knapsack when she felt the mild jolt signaling the end of the tether.

Marco was thrilled with the results, but he decided that more training was necessary. He needed a few more days, at least, to ascertain that he could execute the getaway.

"What would happen if in training, Simidar grabbed the loaded knapsack and flew out of the ledge without the string? Would the eagle continue her flight indefinitely without it?" he wondered.

After careful thought, he speculated that without the string, the eagle would continue to fly with the knapsack clamped in her claws and would return to her home on the ledge at some point. Whether or not she would bring back the knapsack was anybody's guess. Therefore, Marco must continue to use the string on every drill, or risk losing his knapsack. The knapsack was a vital tool for his planned escape. It also served as armor to protect him from the sharp claws of the eagles.

The huge predators were hugged by Marco to show his deep appreciation for the tough, daily training they were going through. The eagles often showed him positive responses.

Hannibal flew out to hunt. Marco looked up above for help, and asked for a prey he would want to share with the predators; Anything but snakes and lizards.

Mayor Gene Salvador and his assistant, Cicero Valencia, were driven by Jeep from Santa Teresa to the bus terminal in

San Angelo to take the noon bus to San Antonio.

He and Cicero left on a Sunday so they could start their on-field inquiry on the eagles the next day, Monday, and through the workweek if necessary.

Gene had a few things on his mind to worry about. His contention was that no one had to suffer from the outcome of his decision to expel the predators from their area. That matter lingered in his mind after having read the latest news report about the eagles.

He couldn't sleep on the bus. Nor on any moving land vehicle, for that matter.

Closing his tired eyes, he reminisced about the past, when he was starting his construction company. His father, a retired public works engineer, helped him get started when he introduced him to several people in the construction business. He learned the rudiments of the business from some of them. In recent years, however, he was disenchanted by their modest and varying degrees of success. He felt there was so much more to be reached, given the projects that were available or forthcoming at the time. It impelled him to take his company to the next level.

Buoyed by his tenacity, when he was but halfway through his eighteen-year career in the field of construction, sixty percent of the construction projects in the area had been awarded to his company.

Gene had not achieved overnight success by any stretch of the imagination. It came only after overcoming serious tribulations inherent with the business, as well as learning to bob and weave around its politics—not an easy task.

Civic-minded and generous, he donated sums of money to benefit the less fortunate people in his hometown. No doubt, these qualities contributed in a big way to his success as a businessman, a politician, and a person.

He lived a modest but comfortable life with his wife and two teenage daughters.

Gene and Cicero arrived in San Antonio late that night. They were booked at the Hotel San Antonio, fifteen minutes by tricycle from the bus terminal.

He ate breakfast with Cicero at the hotel restaurant. Later, he called a former college buddy, Vincent Paterno, who worked at the mayor's office. Vincent picked up Gene and drove him to meet his boss, the town mayor, Albert Sarmiento.

The two mayors talked about town politics only briefly. Inasmuch as neither one of them was familiar with the other's political platforms and affiliations, the subject of politics was relegated to the back burner for the time being.

Gene conveyed to Albert his amazement that San Antonio had grown by leaps and bounds since he last visited the town while in college. They exchanged views about their respective communities and industries. From an agricultural town, San Antonio gradually diversified into an agro-industrial town. Santa Teresa, on the other hand, remained steadfast in its growth as an agricultural community.

"Gene, are you passing through San Antonio on your way to other towns?"

"No, as a matter of fact we came here for a definite purpose. I've read an article from the San Antonio Weekly Gazette that huge eagles were reported to have been seen hunting prey in the valleys and mountains near San Antonio," Gene said. "More than two years ago, we had a tenuous situation in Santa Teresa where two huge eagles attacked and carried away domestic animals raised by some of our livestock farmers. We decided to drive them away from their hunting range by force with the hope that they would re-establish in the undisturbed rainforest of the northeast Sierra Madre Mountains. We persuaded the people to go along with the plan via referendum. Our purpose in coming here is to determine whether the eagles seen around this area lately are the same eagles we drove away from our rainforest two years ago. If so, we are interested to know if the predators are attacking local domestic livestock. We may be able to offer help or give advice to your livestock farmers from our experience with the predators."

"The eagles are not giving us problems so far, and I hope it always stays that way. I have not heard of anything close to what you have experienced in your hometown. We are faced with a different and more serious problem. As a citizen and town official, I'm concerned about a boy who failed to return home after he rode his horse and took him to the mountains with his dog. You probably have not heard nor read about the seventeen-year-old Marco Vega, who was reported missing many days ago. I hope that he has camped out with his horse and dog in the mountains and nothing serious happened to him. His family is currently engrossed in a search, and our municipal police are conducting their own investigation. Read this copy of the San Antonio Weekly Gazette that you must have missed while you were at home preparing for your trip," Albert said.

The Gazette reported: *Marco Vega, 17, a biology student at the City of Pines University in Baguio City, has been missing for more than ten days. The student, who hails from San Antonio, Nueva Vizcaya, is an experienced outdoorsman. He was on a trail ride in the mountains with his horse and dog when he inexplicably failed to come home.* Attached is Marco's old picture taken during his high school graduation.

Gene and Cicero spent the afternoon and early evening hours touring San Antonio by jeepney and tricycle, often talking about Marco and the giant eagles.

"Isn't it odd that eagles, allegedly similar to the ones we've seen in Santa Teresa, suddenly entered the scene here and a boy on horseback disappeared without a trace?" Gene said.

"Indeed it is, and it's also strange to hear that eagles exist in these mountains. Your reference to a possible connection between the eagles and Marco's hold-out in the wilderness will have more weight if those predators are found to be the same huge, aggressive eagles we drove out from the Santa Magdalena Rainforest," Cicero said. "Those were giant monkey-eating eagles capable of attacking and seizing very large prey. I would not associate just any eagle with the disappearance of Marco. They are much smaller, and wouldn't be capable of whisking away large prey, much less a grown-up boy. Before we start looking into the subject, shouldn't we first ascertain that those were the huge eagles that we encountered in Santa Teresa?"

"You're right, Cicero. It would make much more sense to associate the disappearance of Marco with the huge and powerful eagles we came face-to-face with. While we know that the huge predators that recently appeared here are not causing problems with the local communities, it would be great to find out whether or not we've sent them to the northeast or the Caraballo Mountains. That's what we came here for."

"Let's make arrangements to meet with the Vega family. Vincent may be able to help us in this regard. Marco's family who are searching for him could lead us to the mountains to do our own investigation of the origin of the eagles," Cicero said.

Strange as it may seem, Cicero and Gene had developed a bond with Marco, a boy they had yet to meet in person. They were energized with a strong desire to help resolve the mystery of his disappearance. Was it compassion? Was it admiration of the boy with mountaineering skills and qualities they could relate to? Was it the mystique in him that compelled the two strangers from faraway Santa Teresa, in their unbridled fervor, to search for him in the rugged wilderness? Or was it their conviction that a link existed between his failure to come home and the coming of the eagles to San Antonio?

The next morning, Vincent drove Gene and Cicero to Albert's office. The men from Santa Teresa were convinced that the ballyhooed arrival of the eagles, if indeed those were the same eagles they had driven away, had a direct correlation with the disappearance of Marco. Even though they may have had strong reservations about it, they felt the need to discuss it with the town mayor, Albert Sarmiento.

While in San Antonio, Gene hoped to spend time helping however they could in the search for the missing Marco.

"Albert, we have carefully thought through and thoroughly discussed the sudden disappearance of Marco. We have no answers at this point, but I have a hunch that I need to act on. I can't give you the details until we have gathered more information and found facts to examine. I'd appreciate it if we can keep this matter under wraps until we are certain we have firm facts and are confident of a breakthrough."

Albert promised Gene to keep it confidential but asked to be involved in the case, inasmuch as this was his own town.

Conversant with town politics, Gene said apologetically, "Albert, please bear with us for the next five days or so. We expect to come up with facts that I promise to share with you as soon as they are in our grasp.

There's a chance that I may be wrong in my initial

assessment, but I don't think there was foul play in this case."

"All right, but please call me if I can be of assistance," he said.

Mayor Gene asked Vincent if he could ask for a day off and drive him to see the Vega family at their farm. "I'll ask Albert right now," he said.

Gene and Cicero were barely out of the Jeep when Amanda approached them, assuming that the men had some news concerning Marco.

Gene and his assistant, Cicero, were introduced to her by Vincent.

"Good morning, Mrs. Vega,"

"Good morning, Mr. Mayor. Please call me Amanda."

"Is your husband here?"

"No. He and my son are not home."

"Where are they?"

"They are in the mountains in search of my other son, who's been missing for over two weeks now. Vincent mentioned that you are the mayor of Santa Teresa. What brings you to San Antonio?"

"Cicero and I came here to see you and the members of the Vega family to talk about your son, Marco."

"Let's go inside the house where we can sit down and talk."

Gene looked around and admired the renovated house. As a construction man, he could tell that a portion of the living room area was sacrificed for the addition of a third bedroom, but left ample space for the transformed living room. The plywood interior and wooden moldings were sanded and varnished with a rich brown hue, matching the color of the mahogany furniture. Except for a cluster of family pictures hanging on a wall, and a painting of The Last Supper attached to the wall facing the dining table, there was minimum décor that was typical in suburban farm homes.

When they were seated he asked, "Have you seen a pair of huge eagles, monkey-eating eagles that is, that are around this area lately?"

He had said he was here to talk about Marco but he opened the conversation with a question about the eagles. "Yes, Marco and I have seen one eagle. There may be a pair out there but they probably were not hunting together when we saw them in this area. Marco was deeply enthralled with the eagle and asked me to buy him a book about the monkey-eating eagles. I bought two books for him."

"Very interesting. Please tell me more about the eagles in so far as what they hunted for food here, their size, and why Marco became so fascinated with them."

"I have no idea what prey the eagles hunt here. I would think it would be similar to what they hunt in the Sierra Madre Mountains—monkeys, reptiles, squirrels, bats, and other birds of prey. I'm sure you have the answer to that question because you live on that part of the island where eagles settled long ago."

"I would imagine they're similar," he said. "What about their size?"

"I saw the predator for the first time and I thought it was huge. Its enormous wingspan must have measured at least four meters when extended. I can't say it's the biggest one I've seen. I have no way of comparing its size with those of other eagles."

"That makes sense."

"We saw the eagle dive from the sky to lunge at prey running in the valley near our vegetable farm. That very much swayed Marco, who was watching the scene from a cliff, to become not only an avid admirer of the predator, but a potential advocate for their conservation. If I may ask you, Gene, why are we discussing both Marco and the monkey-eating eagles in the same conversation?"

"There may be a link between the eagles and your missing son if those were the same pair of huge predators we drove out from their territory in the Santa Magdalena Rainforest more than two years ago. This is mere speculation, though, and it's too early to draw any conclusion without facts to support it. We came here for the purpose of finding out if the giant predators settled here instead of in the intended rainforest in the northeast. When we learned from Mayor Sarmiento about your son's disappearance, and after reading an article from the Weekly Gazette about huge eagles being seen foraging in your area, two questions came forth: were those the same eagles we drove out from our rainforest? If so, were they responsible for the boy's disappearance?"

Neither Amanda, nor any member of her family, ever thought of that possibility. She was shocked but remained quiet and composed.

Checking his watch, Gene asked Amanda if they could come back. after dinner to talk with the rest of the family.

"Yes of course, Gene. You may come back tonight."

"What time will your husband and son be back?"

"About six or six thirty."

"Excellent. We'll be back by seven, then. Thanks for the coffee."

Gene Salvador and company went back to the Vega residence at seven in the evening, at which time the family had eaten their dinner, and Amanda had finished her kitchen chores.

After the introductions were made, Amanda and Toby served freshly brewed coffee.

Vince preferred hot Lipton tea for his beverage. "Taking strong caffeine late in the evening makes me sleepless at night."

Olin welcomed Mayor Gene Salvador, Cicero Valencia, and Vincent Paterno to their house.

"Gene, I was informed by Amanda of your fact-finding trip to confirm the origin of the eagles that were seen in this area, and to determine whether there's a link between the predators and our missing son. While we don't understand why you have to know where the eagles came from, we can't thank you enough for your concern. Anything that can help us find our son is deeply appreciated by the family. You could have communicated with us in any number of ways rather than taking time from your busy schedule to travel to San Antonio. If you have other reasons to visit our town, we would still welcome you and Cicero."

"We came earlier and told Amanda the purpose of our trip here. Before leaving Santa Teresa, I failed to read the news report about Marco's disappearance. We didn't know about the missing boy until Mayor Sarmiento told us about his case. We asked Vincent to drive us here to talk with the family."

Gene recounted their nerve-wracking experiences with the giant eagles in Santa Teresa: the predators' indiscretions that went unchecked for some time, and his bold gambit to drive them away from the rainforest.

"Here's what we have learned about them," he said. "Witnesses have seen the eagles attack animals in the wild, as well as domestic livestock that weigh many times more than their body weight. The domestic animals that have fallen prey, possibly with a few exceptions, neither had the inclination to fight nor the wherewithal to protect themselves against the fierce and strong-winged predators. If pitted against the giant predators, men would fight for self-preservation to any extent, but that might seem dubious, since no one ever witnessed a human being involved in an attack by a monkey-eating eagle. Like most birds, if not all, they protect their territory from intruders, including humans, and particularly when fledging. Whilst Cicero and I continue to talk about the presumed link between Marco's disappearance and the emergence of huge eagles capable of grabbing large prey, we would like to leave our views in the confines of this home, and not be jumping to conclusions, until we find facts to support them. First and foremost, we'd like to know where those eagles came from. Only then will we be able to provide you with better advice on what might have happened to Marco.

"I invited Cicero to join me here for two reasons. He is very knowledgeable of monkey-eating eagles and had volunteered to travel to the Santa Magdalena Rainforest to drive them away from their nest more than two years ago. While he and the five other hunters were shooting at the eagles' nest to drive them away, he had witnessed the male eagle, slightly smaller than his female partner, suffer an accidental hit in the right wing by a bullet that took out a few of his main feathers. None of the hunters knew how serious the eagle's injury was at the time, but they believed it to be a significant wound. There might be telltale signs of the injury that Cicero would recognize when he observes the eagle in flight or when it's attacking prey. His knowledge of the eagles and the time he spent with the other hunters when they drove the predators away provided him particular insight in uncovering the origin of the eagles."

"We can take you to the forest tomorrow," offered Toby, fresh from his participation in the two-day aerial search. "We may be lucky to see one or two of the eagles during our first trip there."

"Good. Everything's settled for tomorrow then. We'll see you here at around seven thirty, or shall we say eight in the morning?"

"Eight would be fine," Olin said.

CHAPTER 14
HOW THE MAYOR'S GAMBIT PLAYED OUT

The maneuver exposed the predator's underside and wings to Cicero's prying eyes long enough for him to determine beyond doubt that this was the same eagle one of his fellow hunters accidentally shot in the Santa Magdalena Rainforest.

Toby, the pacesetter and field expert, blazed the narrow trail. The three others; Olin, Gene, and Cicero, followed close behind. After they had covered many kilometers of demanding ground, Olin and the two experienced mountain hikers paused for a breather to allow Gene to catch up.

"I haven't done any serious hiking in this kind of terrain in years. I would have kept myself in shape if I had known that I'd be hiking this uphill trail with younger guys," Gene said sheepishly.

"Let us know if you need to rest," Olin said.

Toby and company continued to push through the toughest sections of the route until they reached the end of the southwest trail. Olin and Toby knew that they were closing in on the known monkey habitat when they saw the familiar landscape.

Olin was puzzled as he looked back at the trail they had passed through. He asked Toby if there was any reason for them to follow the long route instead of the more direct path leading to the monkey habitat.

"My intent was to use the planned route but I missed it completely and went the other way. We'll get there, and I expect a smoother hike from here on," Toby said.

"That would work for all of us," Gene said.

When they arrived at that same spot Toby and Olin had regarded as a monkey habitat, not a single ape was in sight.

"The primates do move around looking for food. They are known to be omnivores, but they eat mostly fruits and plants," Toby told the group while they resumed hiking.

They stopped at a clearing when they saw spring water streaming out of a split bamboo channel on the shaded hillside. "This is the place to replenish our canteens and eat our lunch," Toby said, "and maybe rest a little."

"I believe Gene and I need to rest," Olin said.

"Thanks, I need to relax my tired old legs."

"It's been a while since we last saw the eagle. Would you say that was more than a week ago?" Olin asked Toby.

"About that long, Papa. I would say it's time for them to hunt today."

The party continued to hike on in the hope of catching a glimpse of the giant, winged predators.

Toby proposed to the members of the search party that they must pay close attention to the hunted—in other words, the prey.

"The eagles will always shadow the monkeys and other prey to wherever the hunted may lead the hunters," he said.

Cicero recited an adaptation he made from P. B. Shelley's poem "Ode to the West Wind." "If the prey comes, can the predators be far behind?"

"It's strange that neither the hunter nor the hunted have been seen since the previous week. A week's too long without any sight of the winged predators soaring in the sky or perching on tall tree branches waiting for their prey to turn up," Toby said. "Could they have spread out to other foraging areas inside their home range?"

He came to a decision of looking for the monkeys beyond the beaten path. He guided the party to a seldom used gravel road near a small and unnamed rainforest, reaching the site in less than an hour.

A bunch of monitor lizards popped into view when the hikers reached the ridge overlooking the gravel road. The reptiles were basking in the warmth of the sun.

Toby gestured to his companions to move with extreme caution because the monitor lizards were very sensitive to their surroundings. "They can feel the slightest vibration when they extend their tongues, and are adept at eluding people when they sense a presence in the vicinity," he whispered.

The men hid behind a cluster of shrubs while they watched the big lizards sprawling on the road.

From nowhere a giant eagle appeared, snatching an unsuspecting monitor lizard. No one saw where it came from. The attack happened so fast that the men didn't realize what was going on until the predator and its prey were airborne. The lizard thrashed and wriggled to slip out of the eagle's vice-like grip, with no success.

"That was a very daring attack by the predator. I'm impressed," Olin said. "It was so sudden that we were all taken by surprise."

It was already getting late, so the men withdrew from the forest and headed for home. They planned on coming back to the woods to continue their investigative search the next day.

Cicero was disappointed at not having had the opportunity to observe the eagle's right wing. Toby had positive thoughts about their day in the forest, and assured him that they would encounter the eagle again in the coming days, although it might be in a different setting.

Feeling exhausted and famished after the long day's hike, the search party enjoyed warm dinner with hot soup that Amanda had prepared.

Toby reminded everyone that they would stick to the same routine and scour the same general area when they resumed their search in the morning. "There will be a slight deviation in our route after I made a wrong turn today. I learned from it, and I'll be careful not to repeat the same error. We'll take the shorter path next time," he said.

As a matter of convenience, Cicero, who would join Toby and Olin for the next mountain hike, accepted an invitation to spend the night at the Vega residence.

Gene went back to his hotel late that evening. He planned to spend the day in his hotel room to relax his sore legs and treat his blistered toes while waiting for news of the eagles. He expected to hear from Cicero as soon as he found anything conclusive.

The mayor hoped to see his college buddy, Vincent, when he got off work. He planned to invite him and his wife, Maggie, for dinner at the preferred invitees' restaurant. He looked forward to enjoying the cold and refreshing San Miguel beer preceding an appetizer.

The day broke bright and clear. Without ominous clouds

on the horizon, Toby expected a warm and sunny day ahead. "Light rain may develop late in the afternoon or early evening, but we ought to have a comfortable day in the forest."

The three men enjoyed an excellent breakfast made up of fried white rice sautéed with garlic and onions; fried pork sausages; eggs, fried over-easy; and black coffee. Toby and Marco call it "Mama's Breakfast Delight."

The men traveled to the mountains earlier than usual, hoping to cover more ground. They wouldn't need to slow down to keep pace with anyone like Gene, who was several steps behind the pack during the previous day's hike.

They crossed the big valley and took the southwest trail leading to the mountains. They faced the challenging hike across the mountainous terrain once more and began the short ascent to the trail that connected to the old logging road.

Once they were on the abandoned road, Toby paused a moment to decide which way would give them a better chance to encounter the monkeys.

Glancing at a tree that same instant, Olin's attention was grabbed by dark silhouettes that appeared to be moving against the bright background. He rushed to investigate and spotted several brown apes hanging from the bough. Toby and Cicero hurried to join him.

They had learned from previous encounters that monkeys of the brown, long-tailed species were fairly tolerant of human presence. The men sat underneath a vegetated area and waited for the eagles to arrive. They took out their almost forgotten thermos bottles from their duffel bags and knapsacks and enjoyed their still-warm black coffee.

The monkeys demonstrated their vitality by jumping from the top of the tree to a small branch below, bending it to the point of almost breaking it, and then climbing back to the top, one after the other, to repeat the cycle. Toby counted twelve primates, including eight adults. "This wild bunch is loud and boisterous. They're full of energy."

Still sipping their coffee, the trio enjoyed watching the apes engaged in their game of follow the leader. They continued to wait for the winged hunters of the Caraballo Mountains.

Not to be denied their long-awaited and much-anticipated event, the three men were elated to hear a series of high-pitched whistles from the sky.

Then another.

And another.

Everyone looked up and saw a huge eagle riding the rising air current and circling below the cloud cover without flapping its wings.

A second eagle dove from the sky and pulled up, spreading its wings to break momentum, and landed on a tree.

With eyes wide open and hearts pounding, the threesome observed a big scene about to unfold. Like a hawk, Cicero kept a close eye on the eagle when it exposed its underside during its landing. He had noticed that the eagle's right wing appeared normal, with no visible signs of imperfection whatsoever. "It's got to be the female eagle."

Meanwhile, the monkeys momentarily stopped playing and began fidgeting nervously while glancing at the stoic giant eagle perched near them. Settled on a limb and unmoving, the fearsome predator distracted the attention of the monkeys, nonetheless. The apes soon resumed their game but in a more restrained manner.

Cicero's much awaited moment came at last. He gave his undivided attention to the soaring eagle, turned diving eagle, turned attacker—aware that it must very well be the much sought-after male eagle. While he watched the eagle close in on his prey, Cicero was about to learn what he, Gene, and the

Vegas were anxious to find out.

"This is the moment we've been waiting for. It's extremely relevant to the issues at hand," he said.

The male eagle went for a swift attack, seizing the animal with his sharp claws as he pulled up, flapping his wings to maintain balance, and began his long flight home.

The maneuver exposed the predator's underside and wings to Cicero's focused eyes long enough for him to determine beyond doubt that this was the same eagle one of his fellow hunters had accidentally shot in the Santa Magdalena Rainforest.

Cicero was extremely excited to tell Toby and Olin about his important find. "Did you see the main feathers on his right wing?"

"Yes," both answered at the same time.

"It's now definite that those two predators were the pair we drove away two years ago," Cicero said to his companions, who looked impressed with the discovery. "All told, they exhibited the same hunting style, ferocity, and phenomenal size. The missing feathers on his right wing, however, were the true giveaway."

Clutching his prey, the eagle continued to fly back to the nest, while Toby sighted his Brunton compass in the direction of the flight path in order to determine his approximate course. Assisted by Olin and Cicero, Toby plotted the aerial route of the huge bird on his utility map and tied it to a prominent landmark on Mount Malvar—the tallest rocky structure in the area. He checked the data twice for accuracy before he stashed the map in his pocket. The map would help them track the eagles to their nesting site, which was the plan for the next day.

Walking past the trees to the darkened clearing, Toby noticed newly formed rain clouds on the horizon. This formation could be the precursor to impending tropical rains, or even a major weather disturbance, such as a typhoon. Threatening winds danced and whistled through the trees as the resilient branches swayed to and from with the strong gusts.

The men settled on going home right away. They had finished their task, and the sky was becoming gloomy. They would plan their next move early the next morning when Olin convened a meeting in his home.

"My past encounters with the giant eagles seem so long ago, yet they're not easily forgotten," said Cicero. "This event brought back those memories."

The trio arrived at the Vega home late that night. Cicero and Gene attended the meeting there early that morning.

Gene had mixed feelings when Cicero informed him that the eagles were indeed the same ones they drove out from the Santa Magdalena Rainforest. He was not pleased to learn that his gambit had not brought complete success as he had expected; the eagles had not moved to the intended serene and undisturbed rainforest of the northeastern Sierra Madre Mountains. On the other hand, it was not a total failure. Far from that. The two-fold upshot of his scheme, having removed the predators from their hunting range and keeping them safe from the irate livestock farmers, had become a big hit in Santa Teresa. It further raised Gene's stock in the community.

Having determined that the eagles that had dispersed in the Caraballo Mountains were giant predators capable of snatching Marco, a thought Gene could not shake, he suggested to Cicero that if one of the eagles had grabbed the boy, there was a good chance that he was still alive and well inside the eagles' lair. "It's a fact that eagles build their nests on high and inaccessible nesting sites, and there's a good chance that Marco might be in one of those inaccessible places."

Mulling over the boy's disappearance at length, Cicero was in total agreement with Gene in regard to Marco's upgraded chances of survival in the mountains.

Gene opened the meeting by thanking everyone, including his assistant, Cicero, for putting forth a great effort in obtaining vital information about the eagles. "The question that had lingered in my mind for weeks, the same question that brought us to San Antonio, was answered yesterday. Thank God. It's not the result I wanted to hear, for obvious reasons. I'd rather be informed that the predators we've seen here were not the same eagles that we drove out. Still, I welcome the outcome of the investigation. It's a job well done."

Gene reminded the group of the knowledge they'd gained so far: the origin of the eagles, their past habits and transgressions, and the possible location of their nesting site in these mountains. It should help them settle on whether or not the predators had something to do with the disappearance of Marco.

"Why would we put the blame on the eagles without considering other things? I have sought other reasons for the boy's inability to come home: accident, calamity, and the like. Not one choice opened enough argument for me to pursue the notion, having been told of his vast outdoor experiences and capabilities," Gene said.

He offered more feedback with regard to the other issues. "The eagles we're familiar with in Santa Teresa, the same eagles that are here today, are prone to step outside their bounds and create an environment that's fraught with danger or provocation, however you look at it. Those predators are quite aggressive and could attack and carry off large prey. As a matter of conjecture, if they are culpable of seizing and carrying off large animals, why should they be blameless for the disappearance of Marco? Predators don't discern their prey. They grab anything they perceive as food. But bear in mind, as I've said before, that eagles don't have a history of seriously attacking human beings. None at all. I know this will throw a monkey wrench into the whole concept I'm driving at."

"For the past few days, Amanda, Toby, and I have done a lot of brainstorming ourselves," Olin said. "We discussed all the possible reasons why Marco failed to come home after his trek to the mountains. We listed and analyzed the hazards that horseback riders and hikers might encounter in the wilderness, and we didn't find any that would merit our concern. We believe that Marco would be able to avoid all of them. Not that he is indestructible. On the contrary, he could be in serious trouble due to his daring and inquiring nature. Falling off a cliff would present grave concern; but the purpose of his trip, as far as we know, does not include mountain climbing. It is of note to reflect that we are fortunate not to have dangerous wild animals in these mountains. Neither do we have freezing weather, nor snow-capped peaks to challenge. And thanks to the tropical rains, there were no wildfires to contend with early into the rainy season.

He maintained that Marco is intelligent and independent-minded.

"Time and again he demonstrated that when push comes to shove, he will not stop at anything to pull through any exigencies that may come his way. He practically grew up in these mountains and is quite familiar with the common and most adverse of conditions in these parts this time of the year; the unforgiving inclement weather."

"What we hadn't considered to be the reason for his hold-out in the mountains, however, is the possibility that he was snatched by a large, winged predator, as previously speculated upon here in this house," Amanda said. "Up until a few days ago, before we met you and Cicero, this possibility had never crossed our minds. We didn't even know that huge monkey-eating eagles existed in this area up until three weeks ago, when we saw one of them catch prey in the valley."

The group was unanimous on carrying out, once and for all, a thorough search of the eagles' territory. They would track them down to their nest for the purpose of seeking clues that might lead them to Marco.

"It's been almost a month now since his disappearance. We have to move fast and decisively," Olin implored the group.

CHAPTER 15
THE LINK

*Is there a link between Marco's mysterious disappearance
in the wilderness and the eagles' emergence in the
area? Or is it just plain speculation?*

After packing their camping equipment, food, and
various supplies, the trio of Olin, Toby, and Cicero left
the Vega farm at noon. His previous experience with a
similar mission involving the same eagles still fresh in his mind,
Cicero was confident that they were up to the challenge they
faced, even though they'd be searching for the eagles' nesting
place in a different mountain range. He shared good knowledge
of the area with Toby and Olin. After having determined that
the flight path of the male predator transfixed the landmark
previously identified and plotted on their map, they would
focus their search in that vicinity.

Expecting to camp in the mountains for several days until
their project was completed, the trio aimed to resolve the issue
of Marco's failure to come home and its possible link to the
arrival of the winged predators in the area. Locating their
nesting site with the intent of gathering information on Marco
remained the key to their success. It was bound to answer all
their questions.

Gene left San Antonio to take care of routine matters in
Santa Teresa.

He informed Cicero and the Vegas that he would be back in a few days. In his brief absence, he asked that he be informed of any vital development that might arise in regards to Marco or the eagles.

Before they embarked on their separate tasks after the meeting, Cicero confided to Gene his concerns with his extended assignment in San Antonio. He was a bit apprehensive about not reporting back to his construction job with the San Salvador Construction Company. Gene assured him not to worry, because he was on the payroll as long as he was traveling with him. "In reality, your time in San Antonio will be paid by me, not by my construction company. I'll pay you with my personal check. All I ask of you is to assume a key role in the search, and continue to be the productive person you are. With some help from my son Gener, your assistant drafter, Manolito, should be able to cope with the workload in your absence. I expect everything to fall into all the right places," he said.

The weather was getting worse. A storm churning the Philippine Sea was tracked to hit the northeastern coast of the Island of Luzon. It had been expected to land on the coast a couple of hours earlier, but seemed to have stalled somewhere. Toby was neither aware of its intensity nor its presumed lifespan. "It could be a quick-passing typhoon, or it could spin around its general path for a few days or longer before moving on," he said, recalling his past experiences with such weather.

The awareness that an important task lay ahead kept them on their toes. There was no time to waste. They were determined to push on and get the job done, even through bad weather.

Rain-laden wind was swirling around when they boarded their hired jeepney in San Antonio. Midway to Amareto, a farming town thirty-five kilometers north of San Antonio, the road was blocked by a major landslide. "The rain in this area must have been heavy yesterday, judging by this big landslide," Toby said.

"It's unfortunate that our timetable to reach Mount Malvar has been set back by this typhoon," Cicero said, fearing they would have to struggle in the rain to get to Amareto.

The men estimated that it would take upwards of several hours to a day before the road could be reopened. It would depend upon the availability and workload of the heavy equipment assigned to the area.

The storm was gaining more intensity. The sky further darkened as the northwesterly wind blew at an estimated rate of one hundred ninety kilometers per hour. The strong crosswind was whipping against their raincoats and knapsacks, threatening to push them down the slopes as the trio climbed over the landslide to reach the clear side of the road. They commenced to hike the rest of the way to town, praying that the storm would not set off more roadblocks along the way, causing more inconvenience and other delays.

They spent more time on the road than expected, yet they hoped to reach the town before dark. They planned on spending the night there and start ascending the mountain the next morning.

About a nine-kilometer stretch of road separated the trio's current location from the town of Amareto. The wind continued to blow with all its fury, bringing great amounts of rain with it. They felt that they were walking through the worst of the storm. Visibility was poor, but they had no choice but to continue walking. There was no sanctuary from the dreadful onslaught.

Squinting against the blinding rain, Olin's heart leapt with joy when he saw the headlights of a vehicle coming their way. When it was close enough, they saw a passenger on the front seat. "It's a Land Cruiser," Olin said. "The vehicle will have to turn back, with the three of us hitching a ride in the back seats." They were excited with the prospect of not walking to

Amareto and staying out of the storm, even for a short period of time.

Olin signaled the driver to stop. "You can't proceed south because the road is impassable. There's a big landslide blocking it and there's no equipment in sight to open it. Not just yet, anyway. Our hired transportation returned to San Antonio."

"Thanks for the warning," the driver said. "I'll turn my jeep around on that wider spot over there. Where are you headed in this storm?"

"We are going to Amareto. May we hitch a ride with you?"

"Yes, of course...jump in. I'm Michael, and this is my friend, Gus." He opened the tailgate to allow the trio to get in.

To their left, rain-saturated rocks and dirt were sliding down the slopes of the unstable sections of the road, making the trip more daunting than it already was. Though it may be considered safer than hiking by many, riding in a closed vehicle that offered poor visibility was thought of as more hazardous by other travelers. In either case, traveling on these mountain roads during a heavy downpour would always be a big challenge.

The opposite side of the road was just as unnerving to the five occupants of the Land Cruiser. They were four-wheeling on a stretch of road narrowed down by erosion, very close to the brink of the precipice. A minor lapse by the driver would send them crashing to the bottom of the canyon.

Keenly observing the active slopes above, Olin yelled to warn the driver and everyone inside the vehicle: "Look out, look out, landslide coming down our way!"

On the steep slopes, he saw a dangerous mass of rocks and soil that had become loose and was falling down toward the road. It was going to hit the Land Cruiser!

The driver was quick to respond to Olin's warning. He

floored the gas pedal in a desperate attempt to surge ahead and move out from the path of the falling mass. When he took a quick look at the falling debris to his left, he came really close to falling off the road.

Too late! Pandemonium broke loose when the huge chunk of earth and rocks struck the rear of the vehicle with such force it was thrown sideways and off the road.

The five occupants of the vehicle tumbled and bounced inside while it rolled down on the muddy and slippery slope. On its third roll, the Land Cruiser hit a tree stump and lurched upward, throwing Olin out of the open tailgate and into its path.

Looking above, Olin saw the rolling vehicle about to crush him where he had landed. His sheer will to live gave him the boost to rotate to his left in just the split of a second. He had freed himself from his helpless prone position, and thus allowed his legs to catapult his body forward. He tumbled head-first to get out of danger, but slid down the muddy ravine, colliding with a tree. He was knocked out of consciousness.

The Toyota Land Cruiser, meanwhile, hit a large conifer and keeled over to a complete stop. The tree, standing in the jeep's path, had stopped its plunge toward the bottom of the canyon, much to the relief of the four men still inside.

Toby and Cicero left the wreckage in a hurry to search for Olin. They found him lying next to a tree above the wreckage. He was coming to, but was grimacing in pain. "I hit my left shoulder and left knee against the tree. I hope I didn't break a bone," he said.

Toby checked Olin's shoulder and knee and didn't feel any broken bone or dislocation. The ranges of movement of his injured arm and knee were normal. Toby expected him to fully recover from his injuries, barring unforeseen complications or hairline fractures that could not be detected by feel alone.

"We'll have those joints checked by a doctor in San Antonio when we get home," Toby said.

Except for Olin, everyone was lucky to emerge from the wreckage with only minor bruises and bumps.

Toby and Cicero recovered their duffel bags and knapsacks from the damaged vehicle.

"What will you do now?" Olin asked Michael.

"We'll hike our way back to town as soon as we recover our travel bags and other stuff. I'll report the accident to my insurance underwriter tomorrow and we'll decide what to do next. I'm sure my Cruiser's been totaled. Take care of that shoulder and knee."

"I will, and thanks a lot. I hope our paths cross again, in better times. My name's Olin."

"I know of a high school building hall where we can spend the night. I'm acquainted with the custodian who is in charge of it. He loves to hike and camp in the mountains, too, and that's where Marco and I met him. His name is Ray Nicolas, and he lives with his family near the school building. He may let us spend the night in the hall, especially if he learns that we're here in search of Marco," Toby said.

"Great. Heaven knows we need a refuge from the storm: a place to wash up, hang our wet clothes to dry, and rest and recuperate from our injuries. With all the dirt and mess around us, I'd rather spend the night in the hall and not in a hotel," Olin said.

"I say amen to that," Cicero said.

After their road mishap, the men decided to let the storm pass, at least for the night, before they resumed their task.

The typhoon raged all night and continued into the early morning hours. The storm winds buffeted the windows and rattled the galvanized corrugated roof of the hall that was attached to the Amareto High School building.

Toby was concerned about the unsettling noise but Cicero, being a construction man, allayed his fears by assuring him that the school building and all of its parts appeared structurally sound, and able to hold up against the storm.

At daybreak, the men reflected on the path not taken, the rugged but safer route from the big valley through the old logging road leading north to the landmark known as Mount Malvar.

Toby had picked the alternate route and voiced support of his choice to his companions. "We could have saved time and effort by using land transportation to cover the thirty-five-kilometer distance from San Antonio to Amareto. We would then have ascended the mountain trail on foot to connect with the landmark in just half a day's hike, provided we started the climb early enough to avoid camping en route. Traveling by way of the other path we didn't take would have required much more energy; a full day's hike to reach the landmark."

"But if we took the old logging road route, we could have avoided the hassles associated with land transportation in this bad weather," Olin said.

"That's true, but without the typhoon, the landslide, the accident, and other unexpected delays, we could have reached Mount Malvar en route to the eagles' home territory even sooner, and with less energy spent," Toby said. "But I agree with you on the unexpected hassles that you mentioned. After all, we hiked that trail a few times without trouble. I'm sorry, Papa, but unfortunate events do happen when we least expect them."

"As the saying goes; when it rains, it pours," Cicero interposed, patting Olin's good right shoulder.

The weather improved considerably by mid-morning. The rain eased somewhat, but the sun was still concealed by the threatening clouds. Much later, when the howling winds died down, there was a hint of calm settling in and would hopefully last until their project ended. Or until storm clouds gathered once more.

Olin's injured shoulder was wrapped in cravat bandages and his knee was in a splint. He had lost sleep during the night because of his pain, even though he took a couple of aspirins.

Toby suggested that his father stay in a hotel while waiting for the road to be reopened. He could go back home when the landslide cleared. "Mama can apply treatment to your shoulder and knee and take you to San Antonio General Hospital for x-rays."

"What are you talking about? There's no way you're taking me off the task of finding out what happened to my son. I'm not seriously injured, and I can walk, despite the limp," Olin said, his voice quivering in his disappointment.

"Papa, please understand that Cicero and I will be able to walk faster and accomplish more without you to worry about. You are very much in pain and could slow us down if you hiked with us. We will ascend the mountain shortly to our planned destination and camp en route. It will be very difficult for you," Toby said, as he continued to beg his father to go home to San Antonio when the road became passable.

It didn't take much for Olin to alter his mind-set about his participation in the search. He backed down for good reason. "All right. Be careful, both of you, and take care of the business of finding Marco. Finish the job we started."

As much as he would have liked to join Toby and Cicero in their search for his son, Olin felt that his beaten body couldn't take any more punishment than it already had. He must stay and rest, giving his injuries time to heal. He would return to San Antonio for x-rays and medical treatment when the road reopened.

Notwithstanding his injuries from the vehicular accident, he knew that his body had taken a heavy toll from his work in the underground mine. Before he was promoted to middle management, he toiled with many others in one of the most hazardous and oppressive working conditions in the world. At the end of a day's work, he had inhaled air laden with particulates, diesel exhaust, and explosives fumes. He was also nearing his forty-seventh birthday. Even when he was healthy, he simply couldn't match the energy levels of Toby and Cicero in ascending steep mountain trails.

Cicero, an outdoorsman in his mid-thirties, might not be considered young. But working in a classroom, and lately in a drafting room, had saved his body joints from the wear and tear Olin's limbs had been subjected to in the mine for so many years.

If he couldn't take part in tracking down the eagles, Olin's wishes, at least for that day, were to get to a hotel, take a warm shower, rest and nurse his injured shoulder and knee, and lie on a warm and soft bed. He would keep Marco in his prayers and try to catch up on sleep.

As bad as things had gone with the weather—the delays and the accident that caused his injuries—Olin felt a glimmer of hope that Marco was safe in the mountains while waiting to be rescued.

He paused for thought. "In my heart, I know that Toby and Cicero are capable of performing the task at hand. They can do more with me out of the way. Toby is only fifteen, but he's carrying out his responsibilities like a full-grown man. I'm so proud of him. The three young men, with Marco included, belonged to an elite group of mountain men in these parts of the island. In my book, they are the best. At the end of the trail, it's knowing what needs to be done that really matters."

"Time for us to go, Papa. Take care of your shoulders and knees and try not to worry too much. We'll find my brother."

Toby and Cicero headed east toward the foothills. They asked a farmer, tending his array of grain crops, for directions. He obliged by showing them the shorter path to the trail leading to Mount Malvar.

They began the tough stage of their task reaching the top of the mountain. The men stopped for lunch and a much-needed rest after hiking for more than two hours. They built a fire to boil rice, brew coffee, and heat their ready-to-eat dry food.

Lunchtime was a good opportunity to catch up on their conversation that was put on hold while they panted for breath, climbing the steep and rugged mountain trail.

Cicero expressed his amazement at how Olin saw the big landslide coming toward them, even though visibility was very poor at that time. "Toby, if Olin hadn't warned the driver of the impending landslide and he had continued to cruise at his normal pace, we could have been creamed inside the Land Cruiser."

"Yes, we could have been buried like skiers underneath an avalanche.

"The landslide hit the rear of the jeep and did a lot of damage, but it spared us to see another day and to continue the job we started," Cicero said.

"Papa, with over twenty-six years of experience in underground mining, had long acquired the habit of constantly looking up at the roof of mine workings for potentially hazardous loose rocks and materials that could fall and cause serious injuries, or even death. With the similar situation inside the jeep, he had leaned far out from the tailgate to watch the slopes, looking out for signs of dangerous rocks and debris falling. When the vehicle was thrown down the ravine, he wasn't in a stable position, nor was he anchored onto anything fixed inside the jeep. That caused his ejection from the rear," Toby said.

"I never had the experience of working in an underground mine. I've heard that it's a tough and hazardous occupation."

"Papa often told us that although underground work is fraught with hazards lurking in every corner, accidents can be curbed or avoided by taking the right approach: no shortcuts, use the right tools and equipment, follow safety rules and regulations, and have the right mental attitude."

"You impressed me when you decided to take the Amareto route instead of the familiar southwest trail via the old logging road. I'm aware of the advantages in taking the alternate path," Cicero said.

"Thanks for your grasp of the situation. I do appreciate the compliment, especially coming from a seasoned mountain man like you. Marco and I know these mountains very well. The map said we could save time and effort because it was the shorter route. I thought traveling through Amareto would be faster and easier because we could factor in the land transportation net advantage of about twenty-five kilometers. However, that advantage was essentially wiped out yesterday when we were delayed by the landslide and the accident. So, unfortunately, it's back to square one.

They resumed their ascent to Mount Malvar. The path apparently had not been hiked for many months, or perhaps a year or longer. It was covered with brushes and tall grass. They hacked the lush growth of shrubbery while searching tenaciously for visible remnants of the trail.

The sun had set, and darkness seemed not too far off. The duo set up their camp next to the wind-breaking trees and shrubs. They'd be safe from the gusty wind that was threatening to blow across them.

Cicero cleared the dry underbrush and flammable material around the campsite and was about to start a campfire when he heard Toby, who had been cutting dry wood saplings and dead branches nearby, shout in pain. Recognizing the alarming sound of a person experiencing extreme discomfort, he quickly grabbed his machete and ran to help his partner. He saw Toby sitting on the ground, favoring his left arm and wincing in agony. Cicero grabbed Toby's arm and saw a red spot with a small puncture wound on it. Believing that he had been stung by a large wasp, he tried to calm him down, trusting that the pain would gradually subside.

Searching for the wasp he saw a very large, dark-brown scorpion scampering away. Cicero quickly crushed it with the heel of his shoe. Aware of the harmful effect of the scorpion sting, particularly to a person allergic to its venom, he applied a tourniquet on Toby's upper arm and prepared to apply a common first aid treatment to the wound.

He ran back to camp and grabbed his compact first aid sachet, took out his curved, razor-sharp steel blade, specially made for cockfighting, disinfected it with alcohol swabs, and slit the punctured skin. Pressing his fingers around the bleeding wound, he hoped that most of the poison-laden blood was expelled from Toby's arm.

Feverish and slightly delirious, Toby appeared to have

developed a reaction to the scorpion sting. Cicero gave him aspirin for pain, cleaned and disinfected the wound, applied anti-infection ointment, and wiped his sweaty face and arms with a wet face towel to freshen him up. He maintained a warm campfire all night long to give him comfort and to make him perspire as a means of alleviating his fever, and to help eliminate the remaining traces of poison from the sting.

Savoring the comfort provided by the dying flames and glowing embers, Cicero fell asleep in his tent. He woke up at daybreak, surprised to see Toby preparing breakfast.

"All's well that ends well," he said, very appreciative of Cicero for the effective medical remedies he provided him that night. "Maraming, maraming salamat." (Thank you, thank you very much.)

Toby and Cicero reached the area they hoped could provide them with information of Marco's whereabouts. Interspersed with trees and clearings, the ruggedly scenic mountains surrounded the eye-catching pedestal, Mount Malvar, a rock formation rising high above others. Its truncated top showed forth as one of the highest peaks of the Caraballo Mountain Range.

The crag, or tall rock formation, appeared more resistant to erosion than others; hence, it stood apart with its high pinnacle that towered above the surrounding peaks. From a closer viewpoint, the duo perused the landmark they identified with the eagles' flight path they had observed days ago on the southwest route.

"Cicero, we ought to encounter the eagles again in this

vicinity. This site is very near the eagles' flight path marked on our map. When we were conducting the aerial search for Marco over this area just days ago, I saw an eagle fly northward, but it disappeared before my eyes. I have a strong feeling that it landed close to where we are now."

"We have to find their nesting site, and that's the next big thing on our list. I'm almost sure the predators' nest is very close," Cicero said.

"We'll find it. But first, let's locate a suitable place to set up our camp," Toby said.

"The giant birds will notice our presence in the area unless we set up our camp under a thick cover of trees and bushes. They do possess keen eyesight. Fear of attack aside, we need them to continue their daily activities without distracting their attention if we expect to obtain the information we seek," Cicero added.

Climbing to the top of the crag from southern access, Toby and Cicero discovered a breathtaking sight at the northern fringe—a steep cliff that dropped about seventy-five meters down to the broken rock fragments that sloped away from the almost vertical rock structure.

Looking at the cliff from the top, the men could see only vegetation at various layers of the rock wall. The shrubberies blocked their view of the cliff from the top. The duo gaped as they shifted their sight beyond the shrubberies. "Hey, Cicero, we have a panoramic view of the valley below."

Abutted on the north by the rock wall, the wind-swept valley tailed at the base of a hill to the south. "This is the Valley of the Eagles!" he exclaimed.

"The Valley of the Eagles?" echoed Cicero. "That name sounds appropriate, I must say."

The partners had chosen to pitch their tents on a dry gulch

amid swarming foliage cover, not too far from the foot of the cliff. The site offered them an excellent view of the blue sky above, but not much more.

They cut fern leaves and shrubs and fastened them to their tents for added cover.

"Let's keep an eye on the cliff. Eagles build their nests on steep rock walls, ravines, and tall trees," Cicero said.

Their choice of a campsite underneath a thick cover of vegetation didn't provide them a clear picture of the cliff they wanted to keep an eye on. It could be viewed at an angle, but the shrubberies were partially blocking their sight. Their camp was not a good location for observing anything on that rock wall. To transfer their camp twenty-five meters to the west might be helpful, as it would allow them unimpeded view of the cliff. However, without sufficient vegetation cover, they would be exposed to the sharp eyes of the eagles that are known to be territorial. It wasn't a good trade-off. Their choice? Not to move their camp, but to keep a watchful eye on the sky for the soaring eagles and let their flight path lead them where they may. It was only a matter of time before the giant birds would arrive.

Toby prepared their unheated, ready-to-eat food. He couldn't build a fire to warm their food or brew coffee for fear that the smoke would attract the attention of the predators.

Cicero took out his binoculars and began to keep watch of the cliff and the sky above. Marco and the giant predators occupied much of his thoughts while he continued to focus his attention on the mysterious cliff across their camp.

Hours passed. Gazing at the sky, the duo spotted a speck that continued to swell in size as seconds ticked by. Waiting for the arrival of the eagles seemed like eternity, an endless fragment of time that would soon be forgotten the second they realized that their big reward was in the offing. They were thrilled to witness the huge predator emerging out of the blue sky, knowing that they were getting closer to finding the nest, and more importantly, learning the fate of Marco. The duo fixed their sights on the emanating outline of the huge eagle, which caused quite a stir within their hidden camp.

Thereafter, the giant predator began flapping its wings as it gradually descended from the sky in what appeared to be a commonplace landing, similar to that witnessed by Olin, Toby, and Cicero when the big birds hunted near the old logging road.

Its enormous wings braking its dive, the eagle banked slightly to the left to correct its course while it continued to glide straight ahead.

Head-on against the cliff!

The men braced themselves in anticipation of a disastrous collision between the giant eagle and the rock wall. From their limited-view lookout, they were astounded to witness the huge winged predator disappear into the thick clump of bushes on the cliff without creating as much noise as the flapping of its wings.

"Where did the eagle go?" Cicero asked incredulously.

"I don't know! It seemed like it landed on the bushes there," Toby said, equally amazed.

"Or on a nest somewhere on the cliff," Cicero countered. "Bear in mind that eagles prefer to build their nests on inaccessible platforms." He trained his sight on the cliff with his binoculars, his view limited only to what the vegetation allowed, and from his position, the oblique profile of the rock wall did not reveal any amount of information.

Almost half an hour had passed since the eagle vanished into the cliff.

Still peering at the cloudless sky, the duo spotted a second eagle soaring above. The flyer displayed a landing pattern very similar to that of the other predator.

"Toby, look! The eagle has a prey in its claws. Do you see it?"

"Yes. What a sight. It makes me hungry, he chuckled."

"Why don't you have some saltine crackers?"

"I'll have some as soon as we know where the eagle lands."

Clutching its prey, the eagle banked to the left and glided straight to the cliff face as well.

"What's going on in those bushes?" Toby wondered aloud, looking at Cicero, who again had his sight focused on the cliff. "There's something intriguing about the cliff. Both predators flew in, one after the other, and are still there now for almost an hour. Aha! Let me guess. The second predator flew in with their food. They must be very hungry and are devouring their prey as we speak."

"After analyzing all the clues we've seen so far, past and present, I'm now led to believe that their nest was built someplace on the cliff, either on an eroded platform, or the crown of a sturdy shrubbery," Cicero said.

The men snuck out of their camp and climbed the west flank of the crag to reach the top. The intended strategic spot above would allow them to clearly see the eagles below as they flew in and out of the cliff.

Their plan called for Cicero to be hoisted down as far as he could possibly go in order to spy on the eagles, gather as much information as possible, and find clues that could help them determine Marco's whereabouts.

Improvising for lighter hoisting, they anchored the end of a rope to a tree and employed a block and tackle setup to lower Cicero.

"Remember the signals, Toby. One tug of the rope—lower slowly. Two tugs—stop. Three tugs—raise it up," Cicero said.

On his way down, he took extra care not to nudge and loosen rocks that could fall into the bottom of the cliff and reveal his position to the predators, or worse; the rocks ricocheting toward the eagles or Marco with them on the ledge, as they presumed, he was.

CHAPTER 16
ON EAGLE'S WINGS

On mighty eagle's wings I flew
From nest on lofty rock wall ledge
Big valley, I'll return to you …
One day! … It is not mine to pledge.

When it is time, the eagle will
Slip me down to wooded lands
To tread across your earthy till
And frolic on your river sands.

CHAPTER 17
DARING GETAWAY

*You had been deprived of the basic things necessary to
keep yourself healthy and strong, and to make things
worse, you were exposed to the harsh elements—with little
protection provided by the scant vegetation. I'd say lesser
mortals would have succumbed to such conditions.*

D ays ran into weeks on the cliff. Simidar and to some
extent, Hannibal, had been trained to recognize names,
obey command phrases, and understand cues. Their
obedience to command was sound. Constant drills polished
the eagles' skills, and their performances were almost without
fault. It was the culmination of intense and persistent training.

It had rained hard the night before. The raindrops scattered
spores from the wet earth, bringing forth a pleasing aroma. The
scent of moist leaves filled the air. It was early morning and
somewhat cold, as the sun had yet to show up on the horizon.
Marco was up early and preparing for his escape to freedom
with the help of the eagle. "I'll take the plunge today," he
decided. "Today's the day."

There was no turning back now. Marco knew that the
getaway would be the final act, as in a play after rehearsals were
iterated until they were done right. But unlike in a play, there
was absolutely no room for error in this. A misstep could mean
disaster. His aim was to walk home alive and in one piece.

Marco strapped his knapsack snug and tight to his shoulders. He used some of the leftover cotton twine to secure its bottom to his belt for added security, devising a quick release knot to provide him a means of slipping out of the knapsack, and the eagle, if it was necessary during the landing.

He packed the knapsack with light materials such as his extra shirt, his plastic raincoat, and other little things he could do away with, to about two-thirds full. This would provide the eagle with a rounded-out grip for tighter hold of the knapsack during the jump.

There was one last ritual before the getaway. He knelt in prayer and looked up toward the sky to ask God for a safe landing at ground level.

He looked around and made sure that all was in place for the much-awaited escape he had planned and trained for with the eagles for many weeks.

"Lipaaad!" he yelled, using the oft-repeated command phrase he'd employed so many times during daily drills to goad Simidar to fly off the ledge.

Rehearsed a hundred times or more, the eagle took off on cue. The moment she felt the pullback from the string, Simidar turned one hundred eighty degrees and made a shallow but powerful dive toward Marco, who was in a kneeling position with his back against the oncoming eagle. He propped both his arms against the platform to counteract the force of Simidar's lunge from behind. The predator pulled up from her dive and sunk her powerful claws into the knapsack to grab it, lifting Marco from the ledge in the process. He grasped Simidar's massive legs with both hands—a planned but unrehearsed maneuver—as they dropped into the airspace below. Marco was scared but only momentarily, as relief came when the rising air current was caught by Simidar, her enormous wings flapping vigorously as they glided down toward the base of the cliff, seventy-five meters below the ledge.

Cicero was holding onto a rope being lowered by Toby and was almost twenty-five meters down on the west flank of the cliff when he witnessed a huge, brown eagle plunging from a platform on the cliff. Its huge wings were fully extended and flapping robustly.

"What? Hold on a second! A person's hanging onto the eagle's legs!" Cicero shouted. "That must be Marco. I can't believe what I'm seeing. Marco is alive with the eagles! Tobbeee!"

If Cicero's field of sight was lower than the ledge height, he would have seen the full profile of the powerful eagle gripping Marco's knapsack as they plummeted down the cliff. It was a scene to behold, and he missed it by a slight margin.

He tugged at the rope three times to signal Toby to pull him up. When he reached the top, he screamed with joy and excitement. "I saw someone—I'm sure that was Marco being flown by the eagle down to the base of the cliff!"

From his viewing post at the top, Toby saw the eagle fly off the cliff but he didn't see anyone underneath the outspread wings of the predator.

"You saw Marco fly with the eagle?" Toby screamed. "My brother is alive and in good physical shape? Yeahhhhh! I knew it, I knew it!" The teary-eyed Toby cried, "This is real joy. I've always maintained, and I've told my parents repeatedly that he was alive and well. I can't wait to tell them that I was right all along. Yeahhhhhh!"

Grasping the predator's powerful legs, Marco felt her sinews as the eagle tightened its grip on his knapsack.

He had watched a skydiving demonstration when he was twelve years old.

"Is my cliff jump with Simidar akin to a tandem skydive?" he asked himself. "The eagle being the master skydiver and I the novice jumper?"

He had learned that the skydivers had jumped from the aircraft at a preset altitude of four thousand, two hundred meters, or thereabouts, followed by a free fall for sixty seconds before the chute deployed.

What Marco was experiencing at that moment was far more dangerous than skydiving, essentially, because his scheme of escape had never been tried before, and his safety depended on the trained bird of prey to perform a no less than flawless role. Marco knew all too well that a near-perfect execution of the getaway with the wild predator would be unlikely. In carrying out the plan, he anticipated lapses stemming from the timing of the release of his knapsack by the eagle when they were above the expected drop area. He prepared himself for that eventuality.

Simidar flapped her wings briskly to break the momentum when the pair were nearing ground level. Just then, a sudden gust of wind set them adrift southeast of the cliff, far from Marco's expected drop area at the foot of Mount Malvar. When his feet were almost touching the ground, he released his clasp of the eagle's legs, assuming that Simidar would let go of her grip of his knapsack. Realizing that the eagle was still tightly holding on to it, he quickly unknotted the string that fastened it to his belt and raised both arms to slip under the shoulder straps, disengaging himself from the knapsack. He was thrown off-balance and when he hit the ground, he rolled a few times to minimize the impact of his fall.

With cuts over his face and body, Marco was twisting in pain. He was relieved, nonetheless, to have bolted out from the dreaded cliff and survived yet another close call without suffering from any life threatening or permanent injury. Despite his aches and pains, he would be hiking home on his own power before long.

He took out a tattered handkerchief and wiped the blood from his arms and forehead.

The eagle then dropped the knapsack and landed next to him.

No words could describe how exhilarated Marco was to be free again.

He kissed the ground, conscious of his nerve-wracking experience on the high ledge, and the basic things he had been deprived of during the past several weeks. His family, who would be reunited with him in a day or two, occupied most of his thoughts.

Meanwhile, Toby and Cicero swiftly descended toward the base of the cliff via the west flank, springing their feet against the rock wall while they slid down the ropes they had anchored to a tree above. Amid the ensuing excitement from having known that Marco was alive and very likely on his feet, the pair stood in tense silence at the foot of the cliff when he was nowhere in sight. "Where's Marco and the eagle?" Toby asked. "Could he be on his way home as we speak?"

"I really don't know. I'm still trying to comprehend what just happened before our eyes. I've heard from witnesses that these eagles are capable of whisking off prey that weigh several times their body weight. What I didn't hear was that they could also fly human beings, as light as they may be. I thought I knew a lot about this eagle species. The preceding events have revealed that I don't have a complete concept of what these winged predators can do," Cicero admitted.

"Your assessment was based on your past knowledge of the eagles.

That was more than two years ago. Now you've discovered that they can do much more than you previously believed. Perhaps you and I will gain more knowledge of them in the days ahead," Toby replied.

"Knowing that we are in better physical shape than Marco, we can catch up with him if he is on his way home," Toby said. "We'll just have to retrace his route by watching his footprints."

"I know we can join him sooner or later," Cicero said.

Toby and Cicero resolved that their visibility to the predators was no longer an issue now that Marco's whereabouts had come to light. Their clandestine operation was no longer necessary. For the first time since they arrived on Mount Malvar, the partners, sans foliage cover, examined the cliff from a vantage point below the rock wall. With the aid of his binoculars, Cicero found the eagles' nest on the ledge.

"Take a look, Toby. Keep your focus under the thick clump of vegetation on the right and let me know what you see," Cicero said as he handed his binoculars to Toby.

"Hmmm. I see twigs and dry leaves on a platform. That must be their nest. Did Marco live on that ledge for weeks?" Toby asked.

"He sure did. Where else could he have been these past weeks?"

Suffering from throbbing pain and soreness on his face and

body, Marco deemed that it was best to sit and rest until the sting eased off. Then he would begin his long hike home.

Checking out Simidar, who was perched nearby, he realized that leaving them would be quite difficult for him. "There will be pain in parting because of my attachment to them. I must come here and visit them sometime when I get the chance," he vowed.

The eagle flew back to the cliff. As she landed on the ledge, the eagle saw the void left by Marco who for weeks had sat or stood on that same spot. Agitated by her master's sudden absence, Simidar swooped down from the ledge. Hannibal, who had been pecking at the last of his food, decided to follow her.

Toby and Cicero watched the giant eagles ride the rising air current, flying in circles south of the cliff.

"Hear them sound off with their high-pitched whistles?" Cicero said.

"Yeah. And now they're landing. I have a strong feeling that's where Marco is. I don't see any other reason for the eagles to fly there, unless they've spotted a prey in that area."

"If they did, they would have attacked that prey in the blink of an eye and we would have witnessed the action," Cicero said.

"It seems to me Marco doesn't know we're here searching for him," Toby said. "We have assumed he knows we're here, but the fact is, he didn't see us."

"You're probably right... I have the feeling he didn't see us at all. Let's go and check the site where the eagles have landed."

Marco heard voices of men approaching his location. He couldn't be seen by anyone as he sat on the ground behind a big rock he was leaning on. *Are they the drug traffickers still looking for me?* he thought. Without any weapon, and no Gizmo to help him fight the armed men, he stayed calm and hidden behind the rock. He recognized one of the two approaching men when he managed to peek behind the rock. "Toby! I'm here!" he shouted.

"Oh my God, if it's not Marco!" Toby said, running to meet him. They hugged each other. "I've always insisted that you had been surviving in these mountains."

Whatever happened to my brother? Toby thought. He's suffering from fresh injuries he probably sustained during his landing, and they appear to have been treated with cream to stop the bleeding. He's now almost unrecognizable; he's in tatters, his arms and neck are bruised, his face is swollen, and he's showing very little semblance of his good looks.

Their reunion was both happy and sobering. The brothers missed each other more than they'd ever thought. They realized that trekking alone in the mountains could bring more drawbacks than rewards.

Finding the remarkable Marco walking tall and erect, contrary to Toby's and Cicero's prior assumption that he would be too frail to be on his feet, lent further credence to his toughness and his ability to address the problems he confronted in the wilderness, let alone living in harmony with the wild predators.

Introducing his partner and fellow eagle tracker to his brother, he said, "Cicero is an avid hunter with lots of experience outdoors, and who has excellent knowledge of monkey-eating eagles. He taught in high school, but now works in construction as a senior drafter. He lives in Santa Teresa, near the foothills of the Sierra Madre Mountains, and is here to help us in your search. His boss and friend, Mayor Gene Salvador, also joined us in the search, but left to take care of business in his hometown. He is expected to arrive in San Antonio any day now."

Cicero shook Marco's hand, then hugged and congratulated

him for going through a very tough experience virtually unscathed except for bruises, lacerations, and swelling on his face and other parts of his body.

"I appreciate your help. Thanks a lot. I know now who to ask if I want to learn more about the eagles," Marco said.

"Glad that I can be of assistance. It was hectic working outdoors with Toby, knowing that we had an important task to take care of. I'm afraid, though, that I won't be able to teach you anything you don't know about the eagles. In the study of wild animals, I believe there's no substitute for the total immersion you've just experienced with them on the ledge," Cicero said.

"You can both exchange ideas from your separate encounters with the same eagles," Toby said.

"For many weeks, you have existed on the ledge of a cliff, high above the ground. I would presume you were nourished by the eagles' food, because that's the only way you could have survived in that place. You have been deprived of the basic things necessary to keep yourself healthy and strong, and to make things worse, you were exposed to the harsh elements—with little protection provided by the scant vegetation. I'd say lesser mortals would have succumbed to such conditions," Cicero said.

Not one to gloat about his survival prowess, Marco thanked God for making it possible to carry on through the most difficult time of his life. Not knowing how and when his ordeal would end, he avowed that his faith fueled his unending quest to find a way out of the difficult situation he was faced with.

Acknowledging the sacrifices made by everyone involved in the search, he said, "I may never be able to convey a fitting gratitude to you both. But you'll be part of me and my thoughts as long as I live. Thank you very much! At some point, I will aptly thank all the others involved in the search, including Mayor Salvador, my parents, and as I understand, the many yet to be identified."

Questions that Toby and Cicero were eager to ask Marco were put on hold. They had decided to wait for him to open up when he was relieved of most of his pain and felt comfortable talking about his holdout on the cliff.

"I'm sure he'll open up and tell his story on our way home," Toby whispered to Cicero.

Marco glanced at Simidar, who was perched on the branch of a tree not far from where they were seated. Hannibal had taken off to hunt for food, it would seem, since he was nowhere in sight. Despite the pain on his injured and swollen lips, he managed to blow a shrill under-the-tongue whistle that triggered a quick response from the winged predator. She flew the short distance from her perch and landed on the backpack he positioned against his left arm for protection from her sharp claws.

He quickly rewarded the eagle with the last piece of dried meat he kept in his pocket. She took the meat from Marco's hand and began eating it. Marco hugged Simidar and commenced to soothe her feathers.

Both men were astonished to witness the buoyant relationship of Marco and Simidar. How in the world could he have tamed the wild eagle and learned how to communicate with it during his month-long entrapment on the ledge? Cicero wondered. He had only a brief time to accomplish that feat.

Toby and Cicero would fondly call the pair Master and Predator.

In light of what they'd witnessed, Cicero said to Toby that he had seen only the beginning of the incredible saga of Marco and the giant eagles.

Watching Marco give his food to Simidar, Toby opened a can of fruit and offered it to Marco. He ate some, but not much. He was perhaps still adjusting to his newly regained freedom, or maybe he didn't like fruit from a can.

Toby and Cicero prepared to lead the banged-up Marco toward home after they collected and packed their camping gear and other equipment.

Shuttling between his construction company and his job as mayor of Santa Teresa, Gene Salvador was back in San Antonio. He visited Olin and Amanda, hoping to get an update of their ongoing search for the eagles' nest and the missing Marco.

Olin had just been seen by the medical staff at Saint Francis General Hospital in San Antonio. His shoulder and knee were examined, and x-rays didn't indicate any fracture on either joint as a result of the accident. His knee was severely contused, requiring it to be placed in a cast. He was expected to recover fully, although it might take some time. He was advised not to go back to work until he was able to walk without a limp.

There wasn't any fresh news concerning Marco or the eagles from the press or the Vegas.

The feeling of positive anticipation remained at fever pitch. Olin and Amanda awaited word from Toby and Cicero.

The couple had never given up hope that Marco was still alive and well, and subsisting on jungle food. As always, their positive expectations were kept alive and nurtured by family and friends who believed that Toby and Cicero would find the eagles' nest and uncover clues that would lead them to Marco.

Amanda listened while her husband briefed Gene about the typhoon, the landslide, the accident on the road, and his being relieved from the search team due to his injuries.

Olin and Amanda invited the mayor to stay with them in their farm home as long as he was in San Antonio.

"You can stay in one of the two now-vacant bedrooms," Amanda offered.

He gladly accepted their invitation, but he had to get his travel bags and a few personal effects from the San Antonio hotel.

"Will your invitation be good tomorrow morning?" he asked.

"Yes, of course. We would be honored and delighted to have you here in our home," she confirmed.

It was raining hard. Although the sun was still hours away from setting, it seemed late, as the sky was darkened by the hovering rain clouds. Rosie stored her work tools in the shed and was getting ready to call it a day. There was nothing more she could do in that rain. She pulled her raincoat off the rack and remained inside, staying dry until the rain would subside.

In the soaking rain, she caught a glimpse of a dark, crouching figure dashing across the valley toward the vegetable farm. She wanted to scream in fright, but she discovered that she had lost her voice momentarily. Grabbing a pitchfork from the shed, she turned around and waited for the hunkering form that was coming straight at her.

"Gizmo!" she screamed, when she recognized the black and brown family dog. Relieved of fear from the would-be attacker, she ran to hug the canine that had visited her on the farm on most days, rain or shine, when he was not with Marco or Toby in the mountains.

"I missed you. Where have you been? It's been a month since I last saw you."

She and Gizmo ran to the house. When Amanda saw the dog in the house, she screamed with joy and quickly dropped her kitchen chores to hug the wet and hungry-looking German shepherd. She gave him food and water.

In the remote possibility that Marco and Gizmo had arrived home together, Amanda, with tears in her eyes, ran through the door to the front yard, hoping to catch sight of her son walking toward the house past the big valley.

"What's that you're wearing?" Rosie said, holding Gizmo's dark brown leather collar.

"I noticed that, too," Amanda, who was back in the house, said. "Gizmo wore a fatigue canvas collar when he took off to the mountains with Marco."

"That's strange," Rosie said, gazing at the collar with suspicion.

Olin limped out of the bedroom when he heard that Gizmo was home. He reached out and hugged the long-lost pet. "Where have you been? Do you know where Marco is?"

"Did you notice the collar Gizmo is wearing?" Amanda said. "I never saw that thing before. Someone must have attempted to steal Gizmo, keeping him on a leash until he broke loose and found his way home. I'm so glad to see him back."

"I'm just worried, Olin. Aladdin and Gizmo are now home. What about Marco? Where could he be?" she said, wiping the tears in her eyes.

"Toby and Cicero are in the wilderness looking for him. We haven't heard from them yet, so don't lose hope. We can expect to hear positive news from them anytime." His tone was emotional. He hugged her to calm her down.

CHAPTER 18
HOMEWARD BOUND

He survived the harsh wilderness and lived on nature's bounties

On a sad note, Marco bid Simidar goodbye. He hugged the winged predator and gently touched her lion-like plumage. He wished he could see Hannibal, presumed to still be in search of prey, before they left the valley of the eagles.

"Take care, Simidar. I hope to see you again real soon." He tried to articulate a few messages to the huge predator who incessantly gave him her piercing gaze.

As soon as the men started to walk away from the valley of the eagles and the idyllic Mount Malvar, Simidar took off from her perch. While they were waving their hands at the winged predator, she circled around once—perhaps her way of saying goodbye to them. Just when the threesome thought they had heard the last of the eagles' squeals echoing across the valley, they were startled to hear another sound-off as they caught a glimpse of the dark profile of the cliff-bound predator painted against the backdrop of the crimson setting sun.

For expediency, the three men decided to pass through the same route from where Toby and Cicero had come, via the town of Amareto. The path had been picked for two reasons: firstly, to send a wire message to Olin and Amanda the following morning. They would inform them about the good news that

Marco had "escaped from captivity," and that he was on his way home with Toby and Cicero. Secondly, they would cut their hiking distance by utilizing vehicle transportation from Amareto to San Antonio.

The second reason would benefit Marco the most. He seemed to be in the worst shape of his life, despite his claim to the contrary. His weakened physical condition could be attributed to the lack of bodily motion and balanced nutrition from when he was on the ledge.

They checked in at the Hotel Marino in Amareto before midnight. They ordered noodles and soup, some of the easy-to-prepare food, because the hotel kitchen had closed hours before their arrival.

After many days spent in the mountains, and in the case of Marco, weeks of "captivity," their warm bath had been extra luxurious.

Toby offered Marco his extra clothes to replace the torn and soiled garb he was wearing. The borrowed get-up was a tight fit for him, especially the blue jeans being two sizes smaller than what he wore. "They will do until we get home. Thanks," he said.

The following message was wired to Olin and Amanda as soon as the municipal office in Amareto opened for business the next morning.

To: Mr. and Mrs. Olin Vega

Great News. Marco is FREE and WELL.

Coming home with us tonight.

From: Toby and Cicero

The trio boarded tricycles to get to the bus station.

At the bus terminal office, they'd learned from the dispatcher that the earliest trip to San Antonio would leave at 1:00 p.m., and the estimated time of arrival would be around 4:00 p.m. They wished it were earlier, but there was nothing they could do but to wait for a couple more hours.

"Let's find a place to eat before we get on the bus," Toby said.

Staring at the prepared food inside the glass shelf, Marco asked Toby to order more food than they could possibly consume; a repeat of the previous night. Toby believed that Marco's odd conduct, perhaps driven subconsciously, was the result of his past experience on the cliff. He could be suffering from the effects of his recent food deprivation at the eagles' place. *If it's a symptom of a temporary disorder like I think it is, there may be no need to deal with it.*

Amanda, Olin, and Gene were totally ecstatic after reading Toby's wire message they received through the San Antonio Telephone and Telegraph Company.

Patrick, the messenger, on a black Honda Dream 250 motorcycle, was just as happy to find out that Marco was on his way home. He was a classmate and a friend of Toby's.

"Thank God, our son is safe and he's coming home at last!" Amanda sobbed on Olin's shoulder.

Gene hugged the couple and happily offered them a few soothing words. "I knew that Marco was safe and sound in the mountains. I knew it, and I've said it before, but who can make positive assertions without facts to support them? He survived the harsh wilderness and lived on nature's bounties. I'm so happy for Marco and for you, his family," he said.

The rain was pouring when the three men reached San Antonio. They got off the bus and ran to the bus terminal to stay out of the rain. Cicero and Marco sat on the bench while Toby slipped his raincoat on and dashed through the driving rain to look for a vehicle for hire that could take them home to the farm.

Henry Reyes, a high school classmate and another friend of Toby's, recognized Marco and went to welcome him.

"Marco, I'm so glad to see that you're back home. When I read from the Weekly Gazette that you were missing, I immediately joined the search party organized by Jason Santos. We searched for you all over the mountains for more than three weeks. I'm so happy to see that you are well. Jason, your cousin, Jonah, and I found your horse in the mountains, still saddled and in good shape like it never left the corral. We discovered faint footprints it left on the ridge near the Oro Pass. We tracked it and found the horse grazing on the slopes. Jason and Jonah took it back to your farm that evening. Heard from Jonah lately that your dog's home, too," he said.

"Thanks for everything, Henry. I'm so glad Aladdin and Gizmo are back home. I miss them. You will learn what happened to me on Mount Malvar sometime in the next few days. It will be reported in the Weekly Gazette for all of my friends to read and with it, a message of thanks addressed to everyone like you who, one way or the other, helped during the search.

"I'm so delighted to be back in town and be with my family and friends, but for now, I'm tired and I want to rest and recuperate," Marco said.

Toby waved his hand to alert them that it was time to leave, pointing to a jeepney he'd just hired to take them to their farm home in the valley.

Olin was attending an early morning meeting with Amadeo Brown in the latter's mine office. He had made up his mind to resign from his middle management position with the company in order to help Amanda expand their farm.

He was not sure how Amadeo would react to his resignation, but he was ready to parry objections or politely decline possible enticements designed to make him stay.

"Mr. Brown, I'd like to thank you for allowing me to go on an extended leave of absence to search for my missing son, Marco, who is now safe and on his way home. He and his brother, Toby, will be back to their respective schools in a few weeks. I came to tender my resignation to take effect in a month, or if you so decide, as soon as you've hired my replacement. I've planned to work on our farm full-time," Olin said.

Amadeo froze for a moment. He realized that Olin had always been the vital cog that supported the wheel of his ongoing mine expansion project. His departure would certainly create a void in his department unless he could find an equally capable replacement internally, or hire from sources outside the company.

"I'm taken aback by your decision to leave us. What a big surprise! Up until now, I was confident that you would stay and help us manage the expansion project until production time and beyond. Is there anything I or Mr. Gannon can do to change your mind?" he asked.

"I'm afraid not, Mr. Brown. I'm very appreciative of what you and Mr. Gannon did for me, but I must move on and do other things," he said.

"I hate to lose you, but if there's anything we can do to make you stay, will you please let us know?"

"I sure will, but I'm afraid I have already made my decision to help my wife manage our farm. I won't let her continue to do most of the hard work if I can help it," he answered with a tone of finality in his voice.

"All right, I respect your decision. But if you change your mind, we'll leave the door open for you to come back. Who would you recommend as your replacement?"

"Kobi, if you can tolerate his assertive ways, or to put it more bluntly, his cockiness. He can manage the men, and he knows his mining."

"Olin, Mr. Brown and I would like to offer you, for your consideration, a six-month leave of absence, without pay, starting on the day following the date of your resignation," Rich Gannon said after he had a quick closed-door meeting with Amadeo. "Before that period ends, should you decide to return to work here, you can walk through this door and take back your old job without losing your seniority. If we don't hear from you on that day, we'll assume that we have lost you to farming forever. Good luck to you in your future endeavors, be it in farming or mining."

Olin accepted Rich's proposal. He had everything to gain and nothing to lose. He wasn't asked for a commitment to return, and he could get his job back within the stipulated time period if he so decided. It was a one-way proposal designed to work in his favor, if he opted for it, but he already knew the outcome. Amanda needed help on the farm.

"I'm so honored by the attention and generosity given to me by the two mine executives. It's overwhelming. Fair and decisive leaders that they are, they always manage to acknowledge their staff for their minor roles in a big mining operation. This demeanor goes a long way to give comfort and a sense of relevance to people like me, who are recognized for going through the long, backbreaking grind in the mine for many years," he decided.

While he walked away from the mine office for conceivably the last time, his heart was heavy. Olin pondered the shape of things to come as a result of his breakaway from the mining industry.

He dropped by the main office to personally thank Mr. Holly for arranging Marco's aerial search. Amanda had previously sent a letter of thanks to Mr. Gunn and the pilots of the Cessna plane for their role in that search.

When the rain had turned into showers, the sun was sinking on the western horizon. Despite its waning moments, it collaborated with the fine sprinkles of rain to form a double rainbow that seemed emplaced atop the green countryside.

Observing the colorful arcs that appeared to span the length of the valley, Marco noticed yellow ribbons tied around the trunks of trees, mostly pine, lined along the edges of the sand and gravel road. "There must be close to a hundred of them. I'm quite impressed," he said, realizing they were meant to celebrate his safe return.

The jeep pitched and squeaked in protest of the punishing zigzag turns as they descended to the farm.

Marco voiced to his companions in the jeep his deep appreciation of the yellow ribbons and their connotations. He planned to thank all those who were responsible for the display.

When the vehicle finally screeched to a stop in front of the farmhouse, Marco noticed the familiar breeze rustling the leaves of the eucalyptus tree standing next to the awning outside his bedroom. Tied around its trunk was a big yellow ribbon, the largest among all the yellow ribbons he'd seen on the road. It was holding steadfast against the stiff breeze.

"Besides the big yellow ribbon tied around the lone eucalyptus tree, things look familiar around here. The branches of the tree need trimming. I may do that at some point before they start to batter the awning and the windows in bad weather. I was away for a month, but it seems like a lengthier period of time has gone by."

His thoughts were cut short when he saw his parents run through the door, screaming his name.

Toby was pleased that it had stopped raining and the sky cleared, otherwise, it would have dampened the gaiety he expected for Marco's homecoming.

Olin rushed to hug Marco, bad knee and all, while teary-eyed Amanda held Marco tightly in her arms.

"Marco, your papa and I were at our wit's end worrying about you!" she sobbed. "These two good friends, Mayor Gene and Cicero, your brother Toby, your grandparents, and Rosie as well, brought hope to our troubled minds. They constantly reminded us that you were safe and surviving in the mountains."

"I'm very sorry to have caused you all the troubles you went through, Mama and Papa. May I visit Aladdin before I join you inside? It will only take a few minutes."

"Go on, son," she obliged, knowing what the horse meant to him. "But come right back. Your clean clothes are on your bed. We have a lot of things to talk about, but before that we want you to give thanks to everyone who helped us, one way or another, during the month-long search."

On his way down to the big valley to visit Aladdin, Gizmo rushed to meet Marco. He hugged the dog, and they rolled on the wet grass happily. He gently mounted Aladdin bareback and stroked his neck with his hands, but he couldn't take him for a walk, even a short one, because he was pressed for time that afternoon. The team of three—man, horse, and dog—who hadn't been together for a month, had a jubilant but short reunion. He must get back to the house to meet with the people there waiting to welcome him.

"First, I'd like to thank God for the food the eagles shared with me on the cliff ledge," he said in his casual talk to the few gathered in the living room. "To be home again and be with my family and friends was all I could hope for during my month-long absence."

Watching and listening to the lanky seventeen-year-old boy speak from his heart, bearing signs from his ordeal, not one soul in the quiet living room had dry eyes. The cuts and bruises over his hands, neck, and face were healing. He sat on a high stool in a corner, with Gizmo lying at his feet. Rosie and Amanda shed tears in silence.

"My parents and grandparents, Mayor Salvador, Rosie, Cicero, and Toby, who went through trouble and sacrifice to search for me in the wilderness; thank you, thank you so much. I'm forever indebted to you all. I was told that many others were also involved during the long search. I wish to thank them all, too," he said. Stemming more from the fear of boring his listeners than anything, he ended his spontaneous address.

"Can you tell us what happened to you in the wilderness?" Amanda said. "A short story will suffice."

"All right, mother. I'll provide the highlights of the events that transpired in the mountains as you requested. But first, I'll recount that one incident here that led to all the events that followed.

"It began when I saw a giant eagle dive from the sky to grab a prey on the ground. It was the most captivating scene I'd witnessed in my whole life, all seventeen years of it. I'd learned from my mother the establishment of the monkey-eating eagles' conservation program three years ago. It was the first project of its kind in the country, and although it's still in its infancy, it holds much promise.

"As a biology major, I've decided to track down the predator to gain real-life knowledge of the species, and hopefully play a role in the conservation project going forward."

He presented, in a concise manner, every important event as it unfolded, dismissing some of the hazardous incidents and near-misses as mundane experiences that he could have avoided.

Whenever his dog, Gizmo, was involved in the action, however, he proudly announced it without the usual toned-down words. "The sentry's bullets missed me because Gizmo jumped him, locked his jaws on his trigger hand and shook him violently until the rifle was thrown down. I rushed back to help the brave dog subdue the man.

"Toby and Cicero arrived at the scene in time to witness my plunge, with the eagle, toward the valley. It was unfortunate that they were caught in bad weather that caused delays and problems, particularly the accident that had left Papa out of the search, as I've learned from Toby. Had they arrived the day before the jump, I could have used their ropes and pulleys for my safe getaway. Or if they came weeks earlier, I would have been spared the trouble of training the eagles to help me get off the ledge. Even so, they did an outstanding job of finding me deep inside the eagles' territory and helping me regain some of the strength I've lost, with better food, and showing me the easier and quicker way to get home."

He found it ironic that the huge predator that attacked him and caused his fall from the cliff, and subsequently his "captivity" on the ledge, was the same eagle that helped him escape to freedom.

"I have lived through an interrupted summer that was complemented by regular afternoon downpours, strong winds at times, cold nights and mornings, and one of the worst typhoons I've experienced. I have encountered groups of people with different objectives, good and bad. Not a dull moment passed. I have no regrets, and no one to blame for my misadventures but myself. I love the outdoors, and it will always be a part of me. The one crucial lifesaver I didn't have at the time was a longer rope. I didn't have anything aside from the short grazing rope of Aladdin. I'm accountable for not slinging a spool on my shoulder while I was tracking down a giant eagle in the middle of the vast wilderness. Let me tell you that my biggest and heartfelt remorse was having caused you so much trouble worrying and searching for me.

"And last but not least, I'd like you all to know that I thank my mother and the late Mr. Madera for their big contribution in the taming of those wild predators. It did cost Mama a couple boxes of Alhambra cigars and a big bottle of Tanduay rum, but it was well worth it."

Everyone gave him long and loud applause. Despite his youth, he had earned the respect of all his listeners in the room. The group's attention was directed to Marco, and many questions were thrown at him throughout the evening.

In the interim, he reiterated his generous praises to the group for their selfless work during the long search for him.

Toby acknowledged the work of Jason, Henry, his cousin Jonah, and many others who joined the search party. He thanked all who helped, many with names still not known. Everyone would be identified and his or her work acknowledged when Marco would send his message of thanks to each of them through the San Antonio Weekly Gazette.

Knowing that Marco needed assistance in that regard, Amanda asked Toby to fill in for him and get the names of all who would be thanked, and to coordinate it with the Weekly Gazette for publication.

With the help of Rosie in the kitchen, Amanda prepared a delectable welcome home dinner for Marco. The men topped their appetizers with cold San Miguel beer.

After dinner, Marco asked to be excused from the gathering. He needed to retire early to recuperate from the ravaging effects of his stay in the wild.

All evening long he'd suffered from pain and discomfort throughout his body, but he expected complete healing after a few or more days of rest. Earlier, he had been exhausted and ready for confinement to his bedroom, but he forced himself to stay awake and chat with friends and family.

"What about the eagles?" Amanda sneaked the question to Marco.

"What about them, Mama?"

"Are you going to continue to see them?"

"Oh, they are always in my thoughts, and I will continue to see them at every opportunity that arises. I intend to help protect them in any way I can."

Gene and Cicero prepared for their trip home to Santa Teresa the next day. Before boarding the bus that was scheduled to leave at noon, Gene planned to update Mayor Albert Sarmiento with the new developments in Marco's case, as promised, giving the mayor a rundown of the youngster's extraordinary saga as he'd recounted it earlier that evening.

He asked Marco and Toby for a few minutes of their time to talk about the eagles before Marco retired for the evening.

"Would you be willing to join our cause as eagles' advocates? The objective is to help enhance the predators' chances of survival. I've known of your personal commitment to help them, but as a group, I believe we could do more. We can use our own knowledge and our familiarity with the eagles to help the foundation oversee the captive breeding program, and to subsequently release them into the wild," Gene proposed, without going into further specifics.

"I would definitely like to join the eagles' conservation movement that you started in your constituency, and work for their preservation under the captive breeding program. The predators have become very close and dear to my heart," Marco said.

"Consider myself an advocate as well," Toby said.

"Good. I'll be in touch with you both, and we'll meet again in San Antonio in the very near future to discuss plans to help our winged friends in our area of operations. Let's closely monitor the progress of the captive breeding program and determine how we may be of help at this stage," Gene said.

Before he went to bed, Marco raised a question to his father about an issue that had never left his mind since his team departed from the old mill after the storm. "Where is the water that flows out of the Lagrimas Gold Mine drain tunnel coming from?"

"I'm not a mining engineer or a geologist, but I know a little bit about underground water seepages and aquifers. I've continually encountered underground water systems in my twenty-seven years of driving tunnels and mine development work. Tunnels cut through numerous fissures in the rocks. Many of those fissures carry underground water that previously drained on the surface as spring water but now is being diverted to the tunnel and discharged at its lowest point—the portal. Tunnels could disrupt or alter the normal flow of water coming out from underground sources, but they are vital to the mining industry, and must continue to be driven, when necessary," Olin said, with a disclaimer that he was in reference only to local conditions.

"That explains why the creek below the mill was dry. Water is being pulled from the creek to the tunnel below by gravity and is draining out through the portal," Marco decided.

"Good morning, Albert." Gene opened the conversation as soon as he was seated in front of the mayor's desk. "Let me be the bearer of good news in regard to our boy, Marco. He was found alive on Mount Malvar by the two men searching for him, Cicero and Marco's brother, Toby. The three arrived at the Vega farm yesterday afternoon."

He briefly recapped Marco's account of how he had narrowly escaped the cannabis growers' assault, his jump down the waterfalls, his escape from the rat-infested tunnel, his near-fatal fall off the cliff, his ordeal on the eagles' ledge, his taming of the eagles with the use of his bamboo flute, and his eventual escape to freedom.

"You'll read the whole story in the Weekly Gazette coming up possibly in two days," he said.

"Great news! And great story. I appreciate your dropping by my office with this. It's incredible how the eagle attacked the youngster on the cliff, then later helped him off the ledge to freedom. It's really amazing. I'll talk to Colonel Omar Rodriguez of the army detachment unit assigned in this area about the huge marijuana plantation south of Mount Malvar. Those vicious drug growers must be apprehended and prosecuted and their illegal plants destroyed."

"I expect a call from the Gazette sometime this morning for my comments on Marco's safe return. Thanks for the update, Gene."

A news conference at the Vega farm was in progress that morning.

Several reporters and photographers, representing two publications, had been busy at work. After his briefing by Gene, Albert was ready to talk to the media, but he needed to wait a little longer for his turn to say a few words about Marco.

EPILOGUE

Marco awoke fifteen hours after he went to sleep—his first night in his own bed since he came home from Mount Malvar.

Between periods of restful sleep, he had experienced some of the weirdest dreams of his life. In a random recollection of his recent nocturnal visions, the most gripping one that he could remember was his free fall dive into a bottomless chasm. Out of nowhere, a giant eagle caught him and took him to a cliff ledge. He would wake up, and as soon as he went back to sleep, he would be thrown back into an array of chilling episodes that closely resembled the previous ones.

"I've been told that recurring dreams often mirror a person's state of mind. In a sense, they are the extension of one's thoughts, sometimes manifested in a bizarre way. They are, I'm sure, the aftermath of the nerve-racking ordeal I just went through. It's so strange—I was caught in a spell, barren of power to move my limbs."

Checking the calendar hanging above his study table, he realized that it had been ten days since he last saw the giant predators. *"I can't believe it's been that long since I saw them. If I take a short hike to the berry field, I may be lucky to see Simidar or Hannibal there."*

He paused for a moment to reflect on the events that were troubling him lately; the deepening discord in Manila, 450 kilometers to the south. The economic downturn, the need for educational reforms, the growing communist insurgency, and many other issues were causing serious unrest in the capital city.

Massive marches and demonstrations continued to rock the city. Molotov cocktails exploded on the streets, and for a number of weeks the month prior, burning and destruction of properties typified the hostilities there. He hoped the chaos would not spill over elsewhere in the country, as violent protests were portents of a growing conflict. He kept himself informed of the tense situation there, fearful that similar uprisings in Baguio, or other cities, would add fuel to the dire situation in the country. If hostilities remain unabated, the imposition of martial law was said to be imminent.

Good News! That morning, San Antonio Mayor Sarmiento was pleased to read a front-page news report from the Weekly Gazette stating that Lieutenant Luis Gabaldon of the army detachment unit in the area led a team of battle-hardened soldiers, along with handpicked civilians, on a surveillance mission to investigate reports of the existence of a large marijuana plantation in the area south of Mount Malvar. The following day, the same mix of personnel plus a score more of handpicked men equipped with machetes and other cutting tools raided the plantation and destroyed the cannabis plants and all the resources that the illegal drug traders used to grow and process them. The criminals, perhaps having been warned of the raid beforehand, were able to escape. "That will put a stop to their illegal business," the mayor said.

Marco and Toby expected to receive a letter or a wire message from Gene in connection with the schedule of their meeting in San Antonio. Marco assumed that it would take place before he and Toby went back to school. He was anxious to know what a staunch eagles' advocate like Gene would bring to the table with respect to the improvement of the eagles' survival.

Since Marco hadn't read or heard of any success the treasure hunters might have had, he assumed that Dick and Hiro were still in the mountains searching for the elusive loot.

His priorities at the moment were to resume his college education at the City of Pines University, to continue his karate training in order to earn his black belt before the school year ended, and to see Rita again. He had hoped that friendship with her would lead into a meaningful relationship.

In the coming school year, he would be a member of the sophomore class, and he expected to continue to be one of the leaders in his department. He looked forward to taking that role.

Toby, meanwhile, was slated to graduate high school at the close of the school year. The brothers would go back to their respective schools in two weeks.

While Marco was in school in Baguio, Toby would need to continue sustaining their piggery. "The business looks very promising," Amanda often reminded them, to which both agreed.

Marco, Toby, Jonah, and their friends had done enough

mountaineering activities for the season. As a group, the earliest month they could expect to return to the mountains would be after the holidays, very likely in mid-January. Marco had decided, however, to make a run to the berry field, or farther out, in anticipation of seeing one or both of the giant eagles.

He crammed his knapsack with the things he would need if he were to extend his stay outdoors: dry foods and essential light survival materials, including a roll of light but strong hemp rope. He may or may not need them, but he would be ready for all contingencies he might encounter there.

Marco brought along fresh chicken meat for the winged predator he might encounter in the woods.

He went to visit Aladdin, grazing in the valley. After he hugged and patted his horse, he gave him a handful of brown sugar he had packed in a brown bag before he left the house.

Walking across the valley and crisscrossing the numerous rows of vegetables, corn, and tuber plots, Marco noticed that during his absence, significant amounts of farm products had been harvested and marketed in the big towns and cities, and most of the empty plots replanted with seedlings from the nursery.

"I've been told that Rosie's doing a great job here, even with little help from my mother. Her accomplishments bespeak of her as a hard-working farm leader, and she deserves lots of commendation, and maybe a monetary bonus." he reflected.

He visited Rosie in the nursery and told her that he would be away for a few days in the mountains. He asked her to keep an eye on Gizmo when she hears the eagle circling in the sky in search of prey. "You may keep Gizmo on leash inside the nursery for as long as it's necessary for his safety."

"Don't worry, I will," she said. "I'll take care of Gizmo when he comes to the farm."

"Thanks, Rosie. I'll see you sometime soon."

Two days before, during his welcome home party, he told everyone at the dinner table that Gizmo never missed a day without wandering around the vegetable farm, and he was afraid that if the eagle happened to be soaring in the sky in search of prey, she might spot her old enemy and attack. "I'm not saying that Gizmo would be helpless when lunged upon by the predator. On the contrary, the dog will fight to the end to keep the eagle off his back. But at the same time, the giant eagle is most dangerous when she's hungry and would not stop at anything to kill and seize her prey to keep herself sustained. It would be a battle of wits and stamina, and the outcome might be quite difficult to predict. I hope that it won't happen," he said.

When he reached the vegetated area where the berries grow in abundance, he heard the familiar whistles of one of the giant predators soaring above in search of food on the ground.

Marco was so excited to hear the giant eagle's shrill whistles again.

The prospect of seeing and touching the predator energized him. "I pray that this is really happening, and not a concluding segment of the recurring dreams I've had. My timing is perfect! I didn't have to wait long for the eagle to show up. I have the feeling that it's Simidar's turn to scout and hunt for prey, but if what I'm hearing above is Hannibal, I'll welcome that big bird, too," he thought to himself.

Simidar circled overhead and snuck up behind Marco. She gripped and heaved his knapsack, and both were airborne in seconds. He was caught off guard; he had expected to re-bond with the eagles on the ground, without returning to the cliff on Mount Malvar. If that's where they were headed, it would be unacceptable. "No, I can't let this happen," he said, forgetting that he now had a rope to help him escape from the ledge if he happened to be dropped there. Watching the landmarks go by, it wasn't long before he realized that they were going south and not headed back to the cliff.

"It's Simidar!" he yelled, recognizing the predator clutching his knapsack. The giant eagle flapped and gained altitude while Marco held onto her powerful legs one more time.

Soaring above the great outdoors, the Master and Predator set their eyes on the dominant presence looming ahead, with its lofty peaks hidden in part by a scattering of white clouds—the towering Caraballo Mountains.

ACKNOWLEDGEMENTS

It's been said that writing is a solitary job for a writer. That wasn't my case. Time and again, I'd asked my wife, Elsa, to give me her input on my writing project, and she always obliged. What's more, she shared her limited spare time with me, offering encouragement and constructive criticism as she followed my progress throughout the writing process. My special thanks to her.

I am grateful for the generous assistance provided by my cousin, Lydia Grybos, and our friend, Richard Olivas. By critiquing my early work, they uncluttered my way to rewriting, expanding, and improving my first draft.

My gratitude goes to Cindi Richardson for carrying out the initial editing of my draft, and to Lee Ann Jackson from FirstEditing.com for the final editing of the manuscript; her feedback, corrections, and insights shaped my project to its final form. I appreciate her excellent work on the overview and book proposal.

Donna Chin took time off her tight schedule to seek advice, on my behalf, from published author Karen Delk, who walked me through the whole publishing process through e-mail. I would like to offer my thanks to them.

Fiction usually evolves from ideas that a writer conceives. Those ideas can be drawn from many sources, not the slightest of which are experiences in places a writer has simply visited or had a deep involvement with. Many years ago, I had the opportunity to work in several copper and gold mining operations in the northern Philippines. My experiences in those places, now far away in time and space, were indelibly etched in my mind, and left me with a compilation of ideas I used in crafting many of the scenes of this story. I wish to thank my colleagues and friends I worked with in that part of the world.

My appreciation is expressed to my old friends from the Japan Karate Association in Baguio City. They had demonstrated their toughness in the gym, yet they were the nicest and purest of friends anyone could ever have.

To my family, my wholehearted gratitude goes to you for being with me when I needed you.

RESOURCES

National Geographic Society. *The Emerald Realm, Earth's Precious Rain Forests.* Washington, D.C.: 1990.

White, Mel. "Lord of the Forest." *National Geographic* (February 2008).

Tharp, Mike, and U.S. News. *Yamashita's Gold, Mysteries of History, The Loot of Luzon.* April 15, 2011.

Nicol, C. W. Moving *Zen: Karate as a way to gentleness.* London: Paul H. Crompton Ltd, 1975.

"Philippine Eagle." Retrieved March 15, 2011. http://en.wikipedia.org/wiki/philippine_eagle

"Luzon Rain Forests." Retrieved May 20, 2011. http://en.wikipedia.org/wiki_rainforest

"History of Baguio." Retrieved February 20, 2012. www.gobaguio.com/history-of-baguio-city.html

"Philippine Eagle Foundation." Retrieved February 26, 2012. http://www.philippineeagle.org/foundation/

ABOUT THE AUTHOR

Eric Gillies Bernardez, MBA, is a writer and mining engineer currently living in California. He has co-written a national symposium paper for his company, as well as many technical reports. His latest endeavor is his novel Interrupted Summer.

Mr. Bernardez has managed several copper and gold mining operations in the mountainous areas of Luzon Island in the northern Philippines. He found the inspiration for his novel in these places, despite the armed engagements between the government and anti-government forces in one of these mining areas. His real-life study of martial arts is also woven into the manuscript.

Eric is an avid reader who loves to visit historic places around the world with his wife. He appreciates Mother Nature's beauty, especially her majestic, winged creatures, the eagles.

www.ingramcontent.com/pod-product-compliance
Lightning Source LLC
Chambersburg PA
CBHW031543260326
41914CB00002B/241